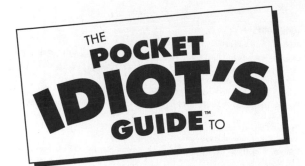

THE POCKET IDIOT'S GUIDE™ TO

Surviving Iraq

by James Janega

ALPHA

A member of Penguin Group (USA) Inc.

ALPHA BOOKS

Published by the Penguin Group

Penguin Group (USA) Inc., 375 Hudson Street, New York, New York 10014, U.S.A.

Penguin Group (Canada), 10 Alcorn Avenue, Toronto, Ontario, Canada M4V 3B2 (a division of Pearson Penguin Canada Inc.)

Penguin Books Ltd, 80 Strand, London WC2R 0RL, England

Penguin Ireland, 25 St Stephen's Green, Dublin 2, Ireland (a division of Penguin Books Ltd)

Penguin Group (Australia), 250 Camberwell Road, Camberwell, Victoria 3124, Australia (a division of Pearson Australia Group Pty Ltd)

Penguin Books India Pvt Ltd, 11 Community Centre, Panchsheel Park, New Delhi—110 017, India

Penguin Group (NZ), cnr Airborne and Rosedale Roads, Albany, Auckland 1310, New Zealand (a division of Pearson New Zealand Ltd)

Penguin Books (South Africa) (Pty) Ltd, 24 Sturdee Avenue, Rosebank, Johannesburg 2196, South Africa

Penguin Books Ltd, Registered Offices: 80 Strand, London WC2R 0RL, England

International Standard Book Number: 1-59257-520-X
Library of Congress Catalog Card Number: 2005938298

08 07 06   8 7 6 5 4 3 2 1

Interpretation of the printing code: The rightmost number of the first series of numbers is the year of the book's printing; the rightmost number of the second series of numbers is the number of the book's printing. For example, a printing code of 06-1 shows that the first printing occurred in 2006.

Printed in the United States of America

Note: This publication contains the opinions and ideas of its author. It is intended to provide helpful and informative material on the subject matter covered. It is sold with the understanding that the author and publisher are not engaged in rendering professional services in the book. If the reader requires personal assistance or advice, a competent professional should be consulted.

The author and publisher specifically disclaim any responsibility for any liability, loss, or risk, personal or otherwise, which is incurred as a consequence, directly or indirectly, of the use and application of any of the contents of this book.

Most Alpha books are available at special quantity discounts for bulk purchases for sales promotions, premiums, fund-raising, or educational use. Special books, or book excerpts, can also be created to fit specific needs.

For details, write: Special Markets, Alpha Books, 375 Hudson Street, New York, NY 10014.

To the people who go.

Contents

What's Going On, and Where Do I Fit In?

There you stand, a thin orange book in hand, realization drifting in like an approaching sand storm. A question forms:

"What am I getting into?"

One minute, Iraq was just a place in the news, safely removed from your quiet life. The next, you're contemplating a move to *the most dangerous place in the world*.

When you go, the thoughts and prayers of your family and friends will go with you, and they'll feel what you do about the place. Or maybe you *are* the friend or family member, looking for a little insight into what your favorite person is going through. I hope you'll read and learn from this book, too, although I'll be directing my advice to the person doing the actual traveling.

You can expect a natural sense of anticipation paired with equally normal feelings of abject terror. Intertwined with the dread will be a slight tingle of adventure. If self-doubt isn't in there somewhere, it should be.

What *Am* I Getting Myself Into?

What you hear about Iraq won't really do justice to the problems you'll see in person. It's a big place, and although it isn't violent everywhere *all* the time, when something happens it happens suddenly. Car bombings, landmines, drive-by shootings, robberies, and assaults are all things you can expect to happen at least once during your time in Iraq. More often than that, you can expect to be frustrated by an inefficient bureaucracy, meaningless schedules, Baghdad traffic jams, mechanical breakdowns, and resignation that seems like indifference among the populace. (And did I mention the heat?)

But although the problems awaiting you are legion, they're also somewhat predictable. Violent groups operate in Iraq. Check. It gets hot in the summertime. Right. The new government hasn't sorted itself out yet? Understood.

Plan to be careful, plan to drink water, plan for delays whenever you deal with officialdom. Above all, have a plan. And remember when you do get to Iraq that you won't be alone.

Your New Best Friends

Estimates numbering the contractors in the Land Between the Rivers range from 50,000 to 100,000. Private security workers are thought to make up as much as 20,000 of those. The number of American troops in Iraq at the time of this writing (late-December 2005) is 160,000 on its way to somewhere around 138,000. There are also journalists, United Nations workers, and aid groups, to say nothing of the vast majority of the 26 million Iraqis who want no part of this war and insurgency mess.

I mention this because those people are now your safety net. Because they deal with the security situation all the time, they have plans for dealing with it, fed by fresh information updated every day. You'll need to tap into that pipeline.

There's a saying among expatriates who live in Iraq or visit frequently: it's a new country every three weeks. I've been to Iraq three times since the U.S.-led invasion in 2003. The training and advice I got in two years has kept me safe in a couple of hairy situations. But more important, it's kept me *out* of a lot of hairy situations. (Knock on wood.) My one wish for you is that you read this, stay aware over there, and come home safely.

The Pocket Idiot's Guide to Surviving Iraq will guide you as you build your own safety net. It'll help you find your way into Iraq, walk you through its bureaucracies, and identify its mortal perils. And it'll help you plan to get back out again when the time comes.

The coming chapters will give you advice on the following:

- Developing a network in Iraq
- Preparing for everyday life in Iraq
- Outlining options for getting around the country
- Some rudimentary strategies for protecting yourself

But it's not bulletproof, and neither are you. Keep this book handy—but keep your eyes open. Things change all the time, and it's up to you to keep from being surprised.

As a crusty ex-British army sergeant major once told me: from here on out, you're responsible for your own safety and comfort 100 percent of the time.

Extras

Practice your new observation skills by watching for a few helpful sidebars throughout the book. They contain key insights about Iraq you might need during your stay.

Come Again

Every once in awhile, new words or concepts will come up in this guide. I explain them in these boxes. Nothing too complicated!

This Just In

Time and money-saving ideas, comments, and reflections from veteran Iraq hands will pop up from time to time. Life's hard enough. Take our advice to make it easier.

Red Alert!

Iraq is an inherently dangerous place. Advice that can save your life or prevent serious injury will appear in boxes like this one. Be on the lookout!

You Don't Say

Not everything in Iraq is life or death. I also include a few case histories, anecdotes, and tidbits of interesting information. When you're telling stories over drinks, or the Iraq edition of Trivial Pursuit finally comes out, you'll be ready.

Acknowledgments

Thanks to the *Chicago Tribune* for trusting me in Iraq and backing up its correspondents' decisions as we report on the war. In particular, thanks to Foreign Editor Kerry Luft, whose counsel on the other end of a satellite phone is always calm and good, and to Peter Kendall and Hanke Gratteau, my bosses in Chicago who let me drop off their staff with such extended regularity. Special appreciation to my Iraqi friends for all the harrowing car rides, lunchtime conversations, and the shared joys and perils. Thanks Marilyn Allen, Tom Stevens, and Jane Fritsch for the guidance on getting this book off the ground. Thanks to Laura C. Brady for the maps in this book (except the first one in Chapter 8). And most of all to the most beautiful and brave woman in the world, my wife, Sarah Brady Janega, for whom I'm a challenge no matter where I work.

Special Thanks to the Technical Reviewer

The Pocket Idiot's Guide to Surviving Iraq was reviewed by an expert who double-checked the accuracy of what you'll learn here, to help us ensure that this book gives you everything you need to know about safely getting by in Iraq. Special thanks are extended to Steven Komarow.

Trademarks

All terms mentioned in this book that are known to be or are suspected of being trademarks or service marks have been appropriately capitalized. Alpha Books and Penguin Group (USA) Inc. cannot attest to the accuracy of this information. Use of a term in this book should not be regarded as affecting the validity of any trademark or service mark.

Iraq 101—7,000 Years in 7 Minutes

In This Chapter

- Catching up on the cradle of civilization
- What the heck happened?
- Who's in charge now
- Learn enough for small talk at a Baghdad cocktail party

Okay, you know the United States led a "coalition of the willing" into Iraq and that the country is a mess now—and you're thinking about heading there, anyhow.

But do you know how Iraq's current problems began a century ago? And more, why it's still so interesting, and why it's so complicated? You will 10 minutes from now.

Where Are You Going?

Iraq puts the "middle" in Middle East and the "hot" in hot spot. A place of rivers in the desert, churning oil wells, and perpetual conflict, it's been disputed ground since humans first domesticated animals and planted grain. To say it's complicated is to say oil is valuable—an understatement.

Geographically and historically, it owes its significance to the Tigris and Euphrates Rivers, which originate in the mountains of Turkey and tumble through desert to the Persian Gulf. Along their banks are groves of date palms, white stucco homes, and beautiful domed mosques.

Iraq.

Whereas the rivers are the source of life and the original attraction, recent Western powers have been interested in Iraq for other reasons—first as a transit point to valuable colonies in the Far East, and later as a source of oil.

In fact, Iraq's borders weren't designed by Iraqis at all—they were drawn by the British after World War I. Those borders now enclose the world's *fourth largest proven oil reserves*. What happens here eventually affects pocketbooks at the world's gas pumps.

> **You Don't Say**
>
> As of 2005, Iraq has the fourth largest proven oil reserves in the world, with 115 billion barrels. The top five, in order, are Saudi Arabia with 261 billion barrels, Canada with 178.8 billion, Iran with 125.8 billion, Iraq, and Kuwait with 101.5 billion barrels. Rounding out the top 10 are the United Arab Emirates, Venezuela, Russia, Libya, and Nigeria. And Iraq has almost as much as Russia, Libya, and Nigeria put together.

Complicating matters, Iraq is making up its government as it goes along and is surrounded by perceived enemies. Under Saddam Hussein, the country, led by its Sunni minority, fought a brutal eight-year war with neighboring Shiite Iran, had issues with its own Kurds in the North and Shiites in the South, and then incurred the world's wrath when it invaded southern neighbor Kuwait in 1990 and lobbed SCUD missiles at Israel.

Moreover, Saddam's government relied on its military and police apparatus. Now that the apparatus is dismantled, hundreds of thousands of Iraqis are out of work, the economy is in the tank, and a vicious insurgency is in full bloom. Even after Saddam, Iraqis are suspicious of Iran's influence on Iraq's Shiite population.

History, Mystery, and Romance

I'm about to throw a lot of names and dates at you, but don't freak out. Just notice how many times *Mesopotamia*—what we now call Iraq—has changed hands, and what a few of its more enlightened rulers brought to the table. Militarily, you can think of Iraq as the Poland of the Middle East—flat, fertile, easy to get an army across, and a generally nice place that other people want.

Come Again

Mesopotamia, from the Greek "the land between the rivers," refers to the fertile plain between the Tigris and Euphrates in modern Iraq and Syria. With abundant water, fertile land, and an acceptable climate, people have thrived here for millennia.

Neanderthal hunter-gatherers lived in Mesopotamia's northern reaches 70,000 years ago. Clay figures and evidence of animal domestication date back more than 9,000 years. The Tigris and Euphrates Rivers have provided a source of irrigation for at least 6,000 years, and cities have graced their banks for more than 3,000 years.

Though settlements date back to 5000 B.C.E., the first civilized people to establish themselves in Mesopotamia were the Sumerians, who in 3000 B.C.E. brought us the wheel, the plow, legal codes, and cuneiform writing on wet clay.

The kingdoms that would follow have a romantic ring to them. (Each is worth studying, though we won't here, sorry.) The Amorites founded ancient Babylon in 1800 B.C.E. The Hittites of 1600 B.C.E. created grand sculptures in Mesopotamia's mountainous north, wrote prolifically, and established the legal concept of group responsibility. Later came the Assyrians and Chaldeans, whose descendents would become Arab Christian groups. Outsiders battling over Mesopotamia included the Persians and the Greeks.

You Don't Say

Even thousands of years ago, Iraq's regional divisions were apparent. The Sumerians founded their cities, language, and culture in the marshy, fertile south. The contemporaneous Akkadians established their own Semitic language and culture farther north.

Something Holy This Way Comes

As in the rest of the Arab world, by far the most defining development in recent Iraq was the arrival in the seventh century C.E. of followers of Mohammed preaching Islam.

Both Mohammed and Islam, the religion he founded, were born in what is now Saudi Arabia. Orphaned early in life but adopted by an uncle, Mohammed married and became a prosperous merchant.

Though religion came to him late in life, it came powerfully. At 40, he started preaching after having a vision in a cave north of Mecca, Saudi Arabia. His teachings, thought to come directly from Allah, or God, are recorded in the Muslim holy book, the Qur'an.

But with enemies in Mecca, Mohammed couldn't stay. In 622 C.E., he fled to what is now Medina, Saudi Arabia, and lived out the rest of his days there. The Muslim calendar began the same year. Mohammed died June 8, 632 C.E., by which time converts to Islam were fanning out through the Middle East. In succeeding centuries, the religion swept from Arabia through North Africa to Spain and eastward through Asia as far as Indonesia. Until the thirteenth century C.E., Baghdad was at the heart of that thriving Muslim empire.

In 638 C.E., Arabs newly converted to Islam swept through southern Mesopotamia to meet the army of the Sassanids (Persians), who had controlled the land for the previous 400 years. Though the Persians had more soldiers and a military machine with exotic weapons that included battle elephants, the Arabs won big. The Sassanid humiliation sent shockwaves through their empire and opened the door to its disintegration within a decade.

For more than five centuries after driving out the Persian Sassanids, Baghdad flourished. It had been at the edge of previous empires. Now it was the center, for a time the richest city in the world. Ships on the Tigris bore treasure from India, China, and East Africa. The *caliphate*—immortalized in Scheherazade's *Thousand and One Nights*—grew rich and spent liberally on the arts.

Come Again

A **caliphate** is the office or jurisdiction of an Ottoman-installed overlord called a caliph. The last caliphate was held by Ottoman Turkish sultans until it was abolished by Kemal Atatürk in 1924.

Still, as Islam matured, schisms in its hierarchy appeared, including the important Shiite schism of 661 C.E. The divisions took a toll. Outlying regions and sects carved away power and prestige from Baghdad, and religious differences that began then between Iraq's majority Shiite and minority Sunni populations still echo in Iraq's power struggles today.

Divided We Fall

Since Islam's schism in 661 C.E., the religion has grown into two sects, the split centered on who should lead the religion after the death of the founder, the Prophet Mohammed.

You Gotta Have Faith

The Sunnis, who make up some 30 percent of Iraq's population (and who ran the place for the past century), believe Mohammed died without appointing a successor to lead his followers. After an initial period of confusion, Muslim elders gathered and elected Abu Bakr, the Prophet's friend, to take the reins.

The Shiites, who make up 60 percent of Iraqis (and who lead the country now after a century of oppression), believe only a relative of the Prophet should lead the Muslims. They settled on Ali ibn Abi Talib, Mohammed's cousin and son-in-law, and his descendents. Ali was assassinated, and is entombed at the shrine bearing his name in Najaf, Iraq.

Amid those struggles from within came pressure from without. The Arab empire dissolved into a series of local strongmen in the twelfth and thirteenth centuries, which led to the growth of tribalism in Iraq.

You Don't Say

Though Sunnis and Shia lived side by side without obvious animosity in the past century, fighting erupted after the 1991 Persian Gulf War after the Shia were encouraged to revolt by the soon-to-depart American-led coalition. The Shia did, but were brutally suppressed by Saddam. More recently, other outsiders have stoked the religious partisanship. Jordanian-born Sunni militant Abu Musab al-Zarqawi made creating a religious civil war between Iraq's Sunnis and Shia one of his avowed goals. Meanwhile, Shiite militias, some members of which were trained in Iran, also have grown violent again. But although the Shia have targeted minority Sunni Iraqis, they've also fought each other for dominance and more strict religious governance.

The Enemy of My Enemy ...

When the Abbasid caliphate, the second of two successive Arab ruling structures, began to decline in ninth- and tenth-century C.E. Mesopotamia, urban society and strong central authority melted away and society turned to smaller functioning units. In those circumstances, the tribal sheikhs emerged.

Like the religious schism within Islam, the arrival of the tribal sheikhs has had a profound impact on Iraq through the centuries. Their power morphed and waned, but has never gone away. The Ottomans saw the sheikhs as a threat and curtailed their power. The British, however, saw value in dealing with rival sheikhs—it was easier to negotiate land rights by playing one off another. Saddam, too, used tribal rivalry to his advantage, securing loyalty by allowing sheikhs to dole out jobs and improvement projects.

This Just In

It's useful to know that tribes persist today, centered in key towns and made up from important regional families. Many forward-thinking sheikhs are even looking to tap into the new government in Baghdad—several have lobbied for titles under the important Ministry of the Interior.

The impact of those early tribal divisions made the place ripe for the picking when Mongols flew out of Asia and laid waste to the countryside beginning in the thirteenth century C.E.

Mongols and Tribalism and Ottomans (Oh, My)

In the following century and a half, Baghdad lay in cinders twice. Genghis Khan's grandson Hulegu, fresh from delivering a serious thrashing to Persia, laid waste to Baghdad in 1258, killed a speculated 800,000, destroyed the House of Wisdom and its library, and dug up the city's elaborate irrigation system. In 1392, not to be outdone, the Mongolian conqueror Timurlane sacked Baghdad again, supposedly stacking skulls into little pyramids as he pulled down every building that wasn't a mosque or a hospital.

Exhausted, Baghdadis had nothing left when the Ottoman sultan Suleiman the Magnificent entered the city in 1534, beginning nearly 400 years of Ottoman rule. Baghdad was the edge of empire once more.

The Ottomans rule laid the groundwork for Iraq's current sectarian divide. Desperate to stop the spread of Shiites from what is now Iran into Asia Minor, the Ottomans used the Sunnis in Iraq's north as a buffer zone. Their governance of the area was just enough to collect taxes and maintain a modicum of stability.

Lawrence! Lawrence! Lawrence!

One of the most instructive characters in Iraqi history, and one familiar to Western audiences, is T. E. Lawrence—the famed Lawrence of Arabia. A hero, right? In the movies, certainly. But in real life, less so. For our purposes, Lawrence is a perfect example of how even good intentions can have long-lasting repercussions in the Middle East—and especially in Iraq.

A war hero for England in the early part of World War I, Lawrence ran British military intelligence agents out of Cairo. Taking advantage of the Arab revolt against German-allied Ottomans in 1916, Lawrence promised future independence and self-governance to the Arabs—which he knew England would never deliver. Nevertheless, Lawrence led Arabs on daring and successful desert raids against the railroads that Ottoman Turks used to ferry supplies.

Despite Lawrence's promises and the Arabs' gallantry, Europe carved up the Middle East after the war to suit their own interests, leaving the Arabs in the cold. It wasn't just that the Arabs had no say in their future, they also felt a measure of betrayal. Among them was Lawrence's best friend in the desert raids, Faisal ibn Hussein of Arabia, who was booted from newly French-controlled Syria and shunned by the newly installed Egyptian sultanate.

I Am the Boss of You

Who	When	Result
Sumerians	3000–2000 B.C.E.	Wheel, plow, writing, legal codes
Persians	539–331 B.C.E.	Beginning of longstanding distrust of neighboring Iran (which was ancient Persia)
Arabs	638–1100 C.E.	Universities, teaching hospitals, modern numbers, algebra, concept of zero

Who	When	Result
Ottomans	1534–1918 C.E.	Divided Iraq into north, south, and central areas, similar to its modern divisions
British	1918–1932 C.E.	Lingering suspicion of Western imperialism
Americans	2003–	Representative govern ment, thriving insur gency

The story had a happy ending for Faisal, but not yet for the Iraqis. London wanted to install Faisal as the first king of Iraq. In an early experiment with democracy, Faisal was "elected" in 1921 with a suspicious 96 percent of the vote. With Faisal in place, rapid Western oil exploration followed, as did periodic convulsions and repression of Iraq's populace.

You Don't Say

Faisal's victory was possible because the Brits kidnapped his chief rival after inviting him over for tea. Nationalist leader Sayid Taleb's populist motto, "Iraq for the Iraqis," troubled the British overseers of the country, so they sent him packing on a forced vacation to Ceylon until the election was decided.

The Arabs never forgot the broken promises of freedom made after World War I by Lawrence, Winston Churchill, President Woodrow Wilson, and other powers at the Treaty of Paris in 1919. Actually, they're still kind of peeved. In fact, anger formed in the wake of World War I molded sentiments still held in the Iraq invaded by U.S.-led coalitions in 1991 and 2003.

Iraq Takes a Baath

The kings installed by the European powers weren't popular among Arabs in general or Iraqis in particular. In 1952, Middle Eastern insurgent groups came out of the woodwork to oppose European-backed governments. One of the most widespread was the Arab Baath Socialist Party. In its ranks was a poorly educated but tough young man from north-central Iraq named Saddam Hussein.

Iraq's foreign-backed monarchy was overthrown by army officers in 1958. Over the next decade, a series of coups in which Saddam participated further rattled the country's leadership. In 1963, the Baath Party in Iraq briefly emerged on top, foreshadowing the firm grip on power they would finally gain in 1968. Once established, the Baath regime of the 1960s and 1970s set up a dictatorship and continued working to promote pan-Arab efforts throughout the region.

> **You Don't Say** _____
>
> The modern pan-Arab Movement grew out of opposition to Israel's 1948 Western-backed creation. It was fostered by Egypt's Gamal abdel Nasser in the early 1950s and 1960s, but has gradually fallen from favor as various Arab states pursued their own agendas. But for decades, leaders in Iraq—including Saddam Hussein—periodically sought to assume the mantle of pan-Arab leadership.

During this time, Saddam climbed Iraq's Baathist ranks, building a reputation as an effective enforcer. He was an unlikely leader, born dirt-poor in the Tigris River town of al-Owja, a suburb of Tikrit—itself just a town with a defunct animal-skin raft industry. But through toughness, determination, and ruthlessness, he made it to the top. His favorite movie was *The Godfather*, he has said, because he admires the fictional mob boss Don Corleone.

Saddam gained popular support in Iraq by reintroducing horse races to the country, previously banned as un-Islamic dens of illicit gambling. (At its core, most of Iraq is a secular place, and it likes its little vices.) In 1979, Saddam rose to absolute power by convincing his friend and president, Ahmad Hassan al-Bakr, to retire early. It's suspected Saddam made al-Bakr an offer he couldn't refuse.

Once in power, Saddam had rivals in the Baathist ranks—real and imagined—killed or jailed. Beginning in 1980, he also embarked on an eight-year war with Iran. In parallel with Saddam's rise to power was Iran's Ayatollah Ruhollah Khomeini, who had overthrown the U.S.-backed shah of Iran in 1979. The Shiite Khomeini's rise had inflamed Iraq's own politically powerless Shiite majority, nudging Saddam to war.

Enter Uncle Sam

During the Iran-Iraq War, the United States entered a marriage of convenience with Saddam's Baath regime. Embarrassed by the coup in Iran, the United States provided Iraq with loans and agricultural and industrial goods, together worth billions of dollars. In addition, America lifted restrictions on outside transfers of military equipment. That meant that at the height of the Iran-Iraq War, foreign arms poured into Iraq, paid for by the oil pouring out. In the end, Iraq's use of poison gas on the Iranian army (and on Kurdish agitators in Iraq's north) brought the Iranian government to its knees. Hostilities ended in 1988, and victory monuments sprang up in Baghdad.

Economically, though, Iraq was badly crippled. Seeking further oil resources to repay war debts—and epically misjudging the U.S. government's true feelings about him—Saddam invaded neighboring Kuwait in 1990. In response, the United States, under President George H. W. Bush, in 1991 led an enormous military invasion that pushed Saddam's army out of Kuwait, but cautiously did not press on to Baghdad to overthrow Saddam.

The decade of United Nations-backed economic sanctions that followed put further strains on Iraq's people and economy, but did little to loosen Saddam's grip on the country.

Saddam's Endgame

Iraq's most recent chapter definitely involves the United States. Citing regional instability after terrorist attacks on the United States on September 11, 2001—and highlighting Saddam's previous use of weapons of mass destruction against Iran and his own people—the United States, under President George W. Bush, led a second invasion of Iraq in 2003. This time, Saddam was ousted, jailed, and as of this writing is on trial for war crimes.

In the former dictator's wake is a bankrupt country unaccustomed to governing itself, leery of Western colonialism, and deeply fractured along ethnic and religious lines. In a nutshell, any government seeking to unite and control Iraq in its present boundaries is going to have a tough time.

Who's in Charge?

If you're one of those people who thinks "the more, the merrier," then you'll love post-Saddam Iraq. There have been three governments (so far), two constitutions, and several plans to rebuild the country and its security apparatus. The goal, of course, has been to create an autonomous and self-supporting Iraq, and gradually the country has been moving toward that ambition.

But since possession is 90 percent of ownership, the militaries of the United States, Great Britain, and other coalition countries have found themselves saddled with the responsibility of overseeing the country as its previous regime faded into the shadows of invasion.

Currently, the fledgling Iraqi government is trying to chart the country's future, beginning with a constitution fair (or fair enough) to its biggest ethnic and religious components: the Shiites in the south, the Kurds and Turkmen in the north, and the Sunni swath between. Among the concerns they must address are how much autonomy to allow each ethnic and religious group. And, by the way, only the Kurdish and Shiite regions have proven oil reserves.

Successive American-backed governments have been navigating the shoal-filled waters of the new Iraq, a procession as bewildering as the country itself. Here, the *Pocket Idiot's Guide* welcomes you to the alphabet soup of Iraqi governance....

ORHA

The Office of Reconstruction and Humanitarian Assistance (ORHA) was formed by the American government in January 2003, months before Iraq was invaded. Tasked with humanitarian assistance, reconstruction, and civil administration, it was led by former U.S. Army Lt. Gen. Jay Garner, the soldier who in 1991 lent assistance to fleeing Kurds after the first Gulf War. Since then, Garner had become president of an American missile contractor and a trusted ally in some corners of the U.S. government.

> **You Don't Say** _____
>
> "We ought to be beating our chests every day. We ought to look in the mirror, stick out our chests, suck in our bellies, and say, 'Damn, we're Americans,' and smile."
> —Attributed to Jay Garner, head of ORHA

Garner created ORHA from scratch, staffed it from more than a dozen offices of the U.S., British, and Australian governments, and waited to be called into action at a Kuwaiti seaside resort as the invasion of Iraq pushed toward Baghdad. (For a few days there in Kuwait, he was my neighbor.)

Timeline: 2003

March 20—U.S. and British forces invade Iraq from Kuwait.

April 9—U.S. troops reach central Baghdad, which crumbles into chaos and looting.

May 12—Paul Bremer made head of the Coalition Provisional Authority, taking over from Jay Garner's Office of Reconstruction and Humanitarian Assistance.

July 13—An Iraqi Governing Council of 25 Iraqis picked by the Americans meets for the first time.

Dec. 13—U.S. troops catch Saddam hiding in a tiny hole near his hometown of Tikrit. He will be charged by a new Iraqi court with crimes against humanity.

ORHA settled ultimately, but briefly, in Baghdad in April 2003. Mostly, it handed out contracts to the outside corporations that still supervise rebuilding in the country. But the office was disbanded on May 12, 2003 in favor of the …

CPA

The Coalition Provisional Authority (CPA) was the temporary governing body designated by the United Nations as the lawful government of Iraq until the country could assume sovereignty. Between May 12, 2003, and June 30, 2004, it was a busy place, overseeing the establishment of security arms, governance, essential services, and economic programs in Iraq.

Timeline: 2004

March 8—The CPA's Iraqi Governing Council signs Iraq's interim constitution.

June 1—Governing Council dissolved to make way for the interim government led by Ayad Allawi.

June 28—Bremer turns over sovereignty to Allawi's government, two days ahead of schedule. Bremer is on a plane out of Iraq that same day.

Aug. 18—A 100-member interim assembly is selected to oversee the Iraqi government and prepare for elections in January 2005.

The CPA moved quickly to put an Iraqi face on the government, under the guidance of career diplomat and former U.S. State Department counterterror chief Paul Bremer.

You Don't Say

"You know, the country is basically peaceful."

"Saddam spent 35 years stealing and wasting money, and all of these systems are very fragile and brittle, and you try to fix one thing and something else gets in trouble."

"I think there really is no shortcut to sovereignty."

—CPA chief Paul Bremer, at various times during his administration

During Bremer's sway, an Iraqi Governing Council was picked (supervised by the Americans), an interim constitution was drafted, and on June 28, 2004, sovereignty was turned over to the government of Prime Minister Ayad Allawi, who sat as head of the ...

IIG

The Interim Iraqi Government's (IIG) sole purpose was to set up elections to seat a body that would write a new (and hopefully permanent) constitution for Iraq.

As a vicious anti-American insurgency took hold within Iraq, the IIG established a beleaguered 100-member interim assembly and prepared for the country's first free elections in half a century.

Timeline: 2005

Jan. 30—Iraq's first free elections in half a century are won by a Shiite-led coalition with 47 percent of the vote. The coalition takes 140 of 275 seats in the new National Assembly. Sunnis mostly boycott the vote, to their later dismay.

April 6—Kurdish leader Jalal Talabani is elected by the National Assembly as president of Iraq. (Kurd-persecuting Saddam was the previous holder of the title.)

July 5—First meeting of parliamentary committee tasked with drafting Iraq's permanent constitution.

Aug. 21—Draft constitution is presented to the National Assembly, but leaves undecided questions of regional autonomy or a time-line for purging Baathists from government.

Oct. 15—National referendum approved Iraq's new constitution, but without Sunni support, and only after supporters in Iraqi assembly agreed to open it to revision early in 2006.

Dec. 15—10 to 15 million Iraqis, including Sunnis, cast ballots for Iraq's first full-term legislature since the fall of Saddam Hussein. But a coalition of 60 political parties, including Sunnis, threatened to boycott the new parliament a week later, claiming vote fraud as Shiite Muslim religious parties appeared to dominate the vote.

Iraq's first elections were held amid jubilant demonstrations across the country on January 30, 2005. Jubilant for everyone, that is, except Iraq's Sunnis.

You Don't Say _____

"All Iraqis will have the right to participate in the government and to ask for their own demands, and this will help to reshape Iraq on a base of national unity."

"All I wanted was to be a university teacher."

—New Iraqi president, Jalal Talabani

The Sunnis decried the interim government as puppets of the Americans, and so boycotted the elections. To the Sunnis' dismay, the National Assembly formed out of the elections was notably absent of Sunni voices.

The United States, arguing that the National Assembly should draft a constitution that will be acceptable to all Iraqis, insisted on Sunni participation in writing it, even though few Sunnis were elected. Talks were fractious anyway, and the future of Iraq's Sunni minority—so long in power under the Ottomans, British, and Saddam—remains uncertain. So, too, is the question of how much autonomy Iraq's Kurdish north and Shiite south will have.

And again, who in the long term will control Iraq's oil? So many questions remain.

The Least You Need to Know

- The region that is now Iraq is one of the cradles of modern civilization.
- Iraq has had numerous foreign occupiers.
- Iraq is unfamiliar with governing itself.
- As efforts to create a new Iraq go forth, the country is beset by a vicious insurgency.

Chapter 2

Boots on the Ground

In This Chapter

- Building a network in Iraq
- Forming realistic expectations for your time overseas
- Gauging the risks you'll face, staying connected to updates
- Developing your plan for Iraq

Now that you know a little about Iraq's history, how will you fit into it? The first thing to realize is that nobody does it alone. Before you commit yourself to moving to Iraq, you should consult with people you know who are already there. If you don't know someone directly, so many outsiders work there now that you'll probably be able to find a trustworthy stranger by reaching out through your family, friends, and working community. Beyond that, there are dozens of resources, websites, and experienced firms available to help you. Because it's such a demanding environment, most people are generous with their advice to newcomers. Take full advantage!

Who Do You Know?

If you're in the military, you'll have the easiest job talking to colleagues who have been to Iraq. The military will insist that you do and provide constructive forums where you'll learn hard-won lessons from the people who went ahead of you.

The goal for the rest of us is to duplicate that ethos of benefiting from someone else's experience. Why? Because compounded mistakes are deadly, not to put too fine a point on it.

This Just In

As you start planning your foray into Iraq, answering a few basic questions will help: what's your profession and what work exists for it in Iraq? An online web search for "jobs in Iraq" will yield a list of companies and contact information. The next question is "What are workers going through?" The source of that answer is the companies you just listed—call them and ask!

To start with: who do you know that's been there? It's a simple question that invites an overwhelming answer, so get out a sheet of paper and a pencil, and we'll break it down together with a handy little chart I like to call …

I Am a Human Rolodex

Question	Action
Who in your business has been to Iraq, seen your work, and liked it?	List their names and contact information. Call them.
Who else do you know that might refer you to someone else or be helpful otherwise?	List their names and contact information. Call them. (Think worker bees, not executives, unless you know executives. We make no judgments about nepotism.)
List friends, relatives, acquaintances, and business associates who have industry contacts.	You sense the pattern. Write them down. Call them.
List places you can go to network—job seminars, professional organizations, social gatherings, etc.	Call them, find out when to go there, how much it will cost, and do it. Unless the other stuff already worked.

If a job service will help you connect with jobs you're interested in, find them online and put those agencies and their contact information at the top of your checklist. It adds a step to your budding plan, but it may be a step you have to take.

In reaching out to your contacts, ask to contact workers they know in the region who'd be willing to talk about their experiences. Most likely, communication will be by e-mail.

When you talk to your future counterparts, ask what a day in the life of their job is like. Are they supplied with helmet, ballistic glasses, and flak vest? Do they wear them on the road? To dinner? To bed? Ask about the pay, how it's administered, how often, and then ask about benefits and how to access them. Don't be ashamed to ask about the vacation schedule, how they get around, living arrangements, and about communication back home.

And above all, ask them if they think those benefits are worth the risk. Then decide if *you* do.

How Do They Live?

A Marine lieutenant colonel I met along Iraq's Syrian border once exclaimed, "Man, Iraq is where you are." It was a brilliant truism, and I scribbled it into my notebook.

At that point, "where we were" was face to face with angry refugees in a desert camp in the no man's land between Syria and Iraq. We slept that night on the roof of an abandoned hotel, covered in dust.

Many others, military and otherwise, spend their entire time in Iraq at one of Saddam Hussein's former palaces, showering daily, playing Ping-Pong each night, and salsa dancing weekly. (True.)

And as the host of a party in my newspaper's Baghdad home (we were filling the pool at the beginning of summer), I once felt compelled to look into the source of nearby gunfire. Martini in hand, I asked one of our armed guards peering through a gap in his sandbagged fortification if the shooting was of concern. The answer: "No, Mr. James, it's a block away, and moving away from here."

I went back to the party. This would rarely happen in Chicago.

Get a Grip

The point is, it's impossible for me to tell you exactly what to expect in Iraq. It varies widely, from place to place and even hour to hour.

One way to deal with this uncertainty is by looking at blogs written in the area where you'll be going. They aren't a perfect source, and you may not agree with their political views, but the good ones give you a feel for how dangerous an area is, or how hot the weather is. (It's a good idea, too, to make sure the bloggers are where they say they are!)

This website offers an interactive map of bloggers in Iraq: acepilots.com/mt/mt-static/iraqmap.html.

Some links on the site drop off as military units and contractors move on. But many bloggers on the map list links to other sites still up and running. Take them with a grain of salt. (Take *everything* with a grain of salt!)

A better source will be people you contact personally while building your own network in Iraq. And *any* government worker, aid worker, journalist, contractor, or blogger in Iraq with a viable e-mail address is fair game while you compose a mental image of what's in store for you.

The Risk Landscape

One thing that can be said for sure is that Iraq is a dangerous place. Experience teaches us that threats there evolve constantly, as methods of killing go in and out of vogue.

For instance, mortar attacks were once the biggest cause of death until insurgents figured out the *improvised explosive device*, or *IED*, which let them kill American troops while avoiding the inevitable return fire.

Since autumn 2004, Iraqi insurgents and foreign fighters have also employed suicide bombers against troops, contractors, and journalists. They're usually in a car heavily laden with explosives. And the IEDs are still around.

 Come Again

An **improvised explosive device (IED)** is a homemade bomb, usually hidden beside or just under the surface of roads. They're typically made of an old 155 mm or 120 mm artillery shell (or two), and detonated by a plunger attached to a wire, or else a mobile phone or similar long-range trigger. A VBIED, for "vehicle-borne IED," is a homemade bomb built in to a car, usually driven by a suicide bomber.

Another persistent threat is that of kidnap. Popular in 2004, the kidnap of foreigners saw a resurgence in late 2005. It's worth asking about while talking with workers currently or just back from Iraq. They may advise you to pick a designated person at home to keep identification photos and personal information—to help identify you in case of kidnapping. Or worse.

To get a feel for what's dangerous out there, you can visit U.S. Department of Defense websites and news outlets that keep updated lists of who has been killed, where, and how. Other groups track the impact of the war on Iraqis and civilian contractors.

Where contractors have died (by city).

It's a good idea to keep abreast of the latest threats to people working in Iraq. One website, Iraq Coalition Casualty Count, is especially useful, because it maintains several searchable databases of confirmed military and civilian casualties since the invasion in March 2003: icasualties.org/oif/default.aspx.

> 98 Baghdad and nearby towns to the south
> 29 Mosul
> 16 Fallujah and Ramadi
> 14 Tikrit
> 13 Bayji
> 8 Samarra
> 8 Basra
> 6 Balad
> 5 Kirkuk
> 4 died after being evacuated to hospitals outside of Iraq
> 2 Nasariyah
> 2 Ashraf
> 2 near Kuwait
> 1 Taji
> 1 Baqubah
> 1 Irbil
> 1 Kut
> Unspecified: 42

Source: Iraq Coalition Casualty Count, as of August 25, 2005

For a taste, let's just single out, by job, contractors ICCC says were killed between 2003 and August 25, 2005. Here are the lowlights: at least 79 companies have had one or more employees killed in Iraq, and 30 companies lost more than 1. So far, the most dangerous jobs to hold in Iraq are "security consultant" (99 killed) and "truck driver" (51 killed).

> **You Don't Say**
>
> The companies with the highest number of deaths are Kellogg, Brown & Root, with 27; Blackwater Security, with 18; DynCorp, with 13; Global Risk Strategies LTD, with 11; and the Jordanian trucking firm Morning Star Co., with 12. They're also generally the companies with the most contractors working in Iraq.

Of the contractors killed, 57 died in their cars or in convoy trucks, another 45 from gunfire or rocket-propelled grenades, 33 from roadside bombs, 30 from kidnappings and subsequent execution, and 29 from suicide bombers and car bombs. Most were Americans (95 so far), followed by the British (31) and Turks (29).

Keep that in mind. If you're an American and KBR offers you a job doing convoy security around Baghdad … just keep the risks in mind.

Tapping Into the Security Pipeline

You can't actually tap into the security pipeline, but your employer should have its own means. If they don't, you should turn down the job.

Obviously, the U.S. and British militaries track what's brewing in Iraq, though daily briefings are generally confined to threats within a certain unit's area. Although that's useful if you're in the unit, security concerns keep that information from being spread too far and wide. The military doesn't want insurgents to know what they know about the insurgency—or how.

Likewise, big contractors keep a daily threat list. But in addition to security concerns, with contractors it's also proprietary, and you won't get daily updates by calling.

However, several security companies compile each day's mayhem into a daily risk assessment distributed to contractors, journalists, or anybody else who pays them for it. The information comes from both the military and large contractors, and the costs of getting and analyzing it are passed on to the buyer.

Getting the Gouge

In the military, "the gouge" is slang for information. We're all starved for good gouge. Here's where to find some:

Strategic Forecasting, Inc.—Sign up for free weekly analyses, which start with facts and move off from there. Sample quote from newsletter: "It is difficult to remember a war of which the status has been more difficult to assess…." www.stratfor.com

Springfield (Massachusetts) Public Library—Links to online news sites, war blogs, background reading, and official government websites. Sample news quote from PBS Online NewsHour: "At least a dozen explosions hit the Iraqi capital Baghdad Wednesday...." Sample blog, quoting President Theodore Roosevelt: "To announce that ... we are to stand by the president, right or wrong, is not only unpatriotic and servile, but is morally treasonable to the American public." www.springfieldlibrary.org/iraqwar.html

U.S. State Department International Information Programs—The official American line. Sample: "Confronting our enemies is essential, and so civilized nations will continue to take the fight to the terrorists," quoting U.S. President George W. Bush. And: "Terrorists have suffered hundreds of casualties and are on the run from an Iraqi city near the Syrian border, a U.S. Army colonel says." usinfo.state.gov/mena/middle_east_north_africa/iraq.html

Council on Foreign Relations—Background and perspective, status of Iraq's insurgency, and papers on the Middle East and North Africa. Sample: "Despite some political progress, Iraq's insurgency shows few signs of waning, experts say...." www.cfr.org/region/405/iraq.html

By the way, all of those quotes came from the same day. Trust no single source.

If you're a journalist—or heaven forbid, an independent worker—it is *strongly* recommended that you find one of these security firms and at least get the daily threat update, if not hire bodyguards and advisors with their help. There'll be more on how to do this in Chapter 7.

The Least You Need to Know

- Seek as many sources of information as possible.
- Talk to people who have been or are currently in Iraq.
- Always compare risks with reward.
- Always, always, have a plan.

Chapter 3

Jobs in Iraq

In This Chapter

- Some of the work non-Iraqis do in Iraq
- A few major employers
- Finding work for yourself in Iraq
- What to expect while working in Iraq

Job hunting in Iraq can lead to some eye-popping moments. Like this one, which might be the all-time best job ad of 2005:

> Available for hire—more than 1,000 combat-hardened ex-soldiers and policemen from Colombia, ready for your private army in Iraq, cheap.

"Dear Sirs," reads the online post at iraqijobcenter. com, under the heading SECURITY FORCE AVAILABLE. "I think you might have an interest in our company and operations …. These forces have been fighting terrorists the last 41 years and are experts in their prospective fields."

(The government of Ecuador soon opened an investigation into the American contractor based there when he posted that private army offer. Seems they're uncomfortable with South American mercenaries being recruited in their country.)

If you're not part of a private army already, it can seem tough landing a job in the Land Between the Rivers. But by reaching out to the network you began building in Chapter 2, you'll find yourself a lot closer than you'd think.

Here in Chapter 3, we fill in the gaps that remain.

Who's Got the Jobs?

Gunslinging aside, there are thousands of opportunities for Westerners to work in Iraq, and even more to do for Iraqis. But all jobs tend to flow through the same four basic conduits of the modern Mesopotamian workforce.

There are journalists, nongovernmental organizations, contractors, and members of several countries' militaries spread all over the country.

First, an introduction to the Western employers you'll find in your neighborhood. Then some advice on how to join them.

The Hacks

It may sound like an insult, but foreign correspondents call themselves and each other "hacks" with pride. If you're unfamiliar with a new country, the first question is always, "Where are the hacks?" You'll be directed to a hotel with an above-average bar for the region. There, over cocktails with gray-bearded old salts, rookie reporters get updates on what's safe, what's not, and where the undercovered stories are.

No one has an accurate count on how many journalists, Western or otherwise, have made their home in Iraq, but I can tell you the number has dropped significantly in the past few years. It used to be a few thousand. Now it's more like a couple hundred. We stay in a few of the famous hotels in downtown Baghdad, and also a few that are out of the way. (The substandard bars throw off prowling kidnappers, who rightly assume the worst about us.) A few news organizations still rent houses. Ask a hack with a Baghdad dateline where they're staying. For their security, I won't get into it too deeply here.

For foreign journalists in Iraq, security is everything, because we don't live on heavily fortified military bases. Mostly we live in lightly guarded compounds around hotels. It's why hacks in Iraq don't get out as much as they'd like, and why Western news organizations aren't letting inexperienced reporters into their Baghdad bureaus. As one old hack told me: "I've been to Vietnam. This is worse. In Iraq, we're hunted."

But there's a counterpoint to those concerns. As the story wears on, a lot of the correspondents who covered Iraq in 2003 and 2004 have moved on to other assignments, while news organizations have had difficulty finding new staffers to take their place.

Red Alert!

The Committee to Protect Journalists says at least 53 journalists have been killed since March 2003 while working in Iraq—15 in 2005, 24 in 2004, and 14 in 2003. Most of them—34— were Iraqis. Of the 53 killed, 30 were killed by insurgents and 13 by U.S. forces. At the same time, 28 journalists (including 2 from my hotel) were kidnapped and released. Two others were abducted and murdered. By comparison, 51 journalists have been killed in Colombia. But that's since 1986. The Freedom Forum says 66 were killed in Vietnam, and 68 in World War II. Be very observant.

If Iraq is a passion for you, and you work for a big news organization, make known your interest in the place. Insist on being trained by a private security agency before you go.

If you're a freelancer, there's less of a safety net. You need to give serious consideration to how you plan to live in Iraq, and to what expense you're willing to go to provide your own security.

The NGOs

Two back-to-back wars, a decade of sanctions, then the 2003 invasion and subsequent looting, insurgency, and criminal activities have put deep strains on Iraq's society, economy, and standard of living.

One estimate pegged Iraq's per-capita income at $500 (in U.S. dollars) in 2000, down from $3,500 in 1991. Alongside that strain has been hyperinflation, skyrocketing debt, unemployment that could be as high as 50 percent, and general fears and uncertainty about the future.

Without a fully formed government to respond, it has fallen to nongovernmental organizations— NGOs, in the parlance—to pick up the slack. The NGOs you'll encounter in Iraq range from gray ladies like the United Nations and the International Federation of the Red Cross and Red Crescent to puckish over-night operations like Circus2Iraq.

Together, 50 or more of these NGOs in Iraq try to close gaps in public education and public health, urban infrastructure, human rights, and the plight of internally displaced people. It's a full plate, and every two steps forward seem dogged by one step back.

If you're idealistic and patient, you may want to join the ranks of the NGOs in Iraq.

It should also be noted that, while still active in Iraq, many have withdrawn their staffs to countries nearby after bombings in Iraq seemed to target them in late 2003 and early 2004. Many keep the bulk of their expatriate staff in Jordan or elsewhere.

You Don't Say _____

In 1859, Swiss businessman Henri Dunant (1828–1910) visited a battlefield at Solferino in northern Italy and was deeply moved to see how war affected the lives and dignity of combatant and civilian alike. The memoir he wrote on the battle inspired the 1863 founding of the International Committee of the Red Cross (ICRC). The group had two goals: to create voluntary relief societies that would care for the wounded in wartime, and to formulate an international agreement that would serve as the basis and support for those relief societies. The International Federation of the Red Cross and Red Crescent that grew from that agreement exists to this day.

Source: American Red Cross, Orange County Chapter

The Contractors

By most estimates, there are more than 100,000 civilian contractors and some 20,000 private security workers in Iraq. The job seekers pour in from the United States, Great Britain, South Africa, South Asia, and Europe. (Possibly even Ecuador.)

Salaries range from $60,000 to $175,000 a year, depending on how old you are, your qualifications, and your experience. Much of that is tax free if you agree to stay for a certain amount of time. Many contractors are former soldiers. Others are lured by the money and promise of adventure in a land desperate for electricity, bridges, and fresh water.

Some get more adventure than they want—truck drivers are in high demand, and Iraq's roads are notoriously dangerous. But most spend a year in-country, living on a single military post, housed in a trailer, doing things such as slinging ice cream to troops in the dining facility or working in the base morale and recreation building.

Show Me the Money

Top 10 U.S. Contractors	2002–2004 Contract Value
Kellogg, Brown & Root	$11.4 billion
Parsons Corp.	$5.3 billion
Fluor Corp.	$3.7 billion
Washington Group Intl.	$3.1 billion
Shaw Group	$3.0 billion
Bechtel Group Inc.	$2.9 billion
Perini Corp.	$2.5 billion
Contrack Intl. Inc.	$2.3 billion
Tetra Tech Inc.	$1.54 billion
USA Environmental Inc.	$1.53 billion
Total:	**$37.4 billion**

SOURCE: The Center for Public Integrity

NOTE: Includes contracts in Iraq and Afghanistan

Between 2002 and 2004, more than 150 prime contractors were retained for more than $51 billion of work in Iraq, much of it in support of the U.S. and British military presence.

The biggest of them all is Halliburton subsidiary Kellogg, Brown & Root—it had more than 700 posted jobs the last time I checked their website, including calls for paramedics, managers, corporate security workers, administrative assistants, and safety coordinators. Jobs at KBR for mechanics, equipment operators, and positions in logistics and maintenance are in high demand and had multiple listings.

More on how to apply for those jobs in a minute.

The Military

As of late 2005, there is talk of downsizing the U.S. military in Iraq. But there are still more than 120,000 U.S. troops stationed there now, and security demands mean at least some of them will need to stay for the foreseeable future.

The largest military presence in Iraq is maintained by the U.S. Army, followed by the Marine Corps, though considerable groups of Navy and Air Force troops also ply their trade there, and even the Coast Guard is at work nearby.

Clearly, the numbers alone show the most common way into Iraq for Westerners—and particularly Americans—is through the armed forces. But because there are good ways and bad ways of doing anything, you should consider your post-Iraq future in the military, too. If you decide to join, lay the groundwork for a satisfying career later.

Be sure you'd fit in before signing anything. Look into whether you're old enough, but not too old. Ask a recruiter for advice on the Armed Services Vocational Aptitude Battery—the math and word test used to recommend you for specialty areas in the military. The higher you score, the better your chances of getting the job you want later. Decide before joining if you want to enlist or aim for the officer corps.

When you're past that stage, it only takes a couple of days to take the ASVAB, get a physical, choose a job, and swear in. At that point, and only after that point, you're in the military. And when the military takes you to Iraq, you and your family are in for a demanding (and frequently rewarding) few months.

Finding a Job

Outside of the military, the war in Iraq has opened up thousands of support jobs with hundreds of U.S. companies involved in a security, logistics, and non-military operations. There are NGO openings on top of that. And if you're an ambitious journalist with good connections, possibilities exist for you there, too.

These jobs aren't for everyone. Employers prefer applicants to be hardworking, conscientious, and skilled. Experience in the Arab world and foreign language skills aren't required, but they're an obvious advantage.

But just like in Hollywood, looking for a job in Iraq can center on who you know as much as what you know. About the only advice I can give you is to stay flexible and informed.

To land a job, you'll have to be experienced, connected, and smart. Reach out to others working in Iraq in your field. Stay up-to-date on current events in your industry. Read as much as possible about who gets government contracts and who has lost them.

And keep an ear out for which employers to avoid altogether!

Job Hunting Resources in Iraq

A web search for "jobs in Iraq" will reveal dozens of websites, some of them loaded with contracting jobs in Iraq. From truck driving to oil field maintenance, job training to water treatment and railway maintenance, just about everything's available in Iraq these days.

If you'd like a more direct path to the contractors, try the biggies:

- Kellogg, Brown & Root, www.halliburton. comz/kbr
- Parsons Corp., www.parsons.com
- Washington Group International, www. wgint.com/opp_iraq.html.

For jobs at nongovernmental organizations, try the following:

- The United Nations Assistance Mission for Iraq, www.uniraq.org/tools/vacancies.asp
- The jobs link at www.idealist.org

Look for more in the Resources appendix!

No Day in the Life

One of the great things about working in Iraq is that there are lots of days that are similar, but not a single day that is typical.

I have seen contractors whose job it was to turn the base dining facility into a sports bar. I have seen contractors who spend a year scooping ice cream. I have seen workers who get up each day and spend their hours scrubbing toilets. And although I haven't met this person, I know there is a truck driver somewhere whose job it is to drive enormous power generators into the country without ever accelerating to more than 10 miles per hour. (Those things can't be jostled.)

To varying degrees, each was vulnerable to attack. Without exception, each was exposed to withering summertime temperatures well over 110 degrees Fahrenheit (43 degrees Celsius).

Most contractors live in air-conditioned trailers on military bases or in the heavily fortified Green Zone in central Baghdad. In the past two years, telephone service, satellite television, and flush toilets have come to just about everywhere Westerners gather in Iraq.

Wherever they are, the days are long. And aside from a couple of weeks off in a typical yearlong contract, things get monotonous, and danger is never far away. Mortars and rockets fall on even the largest of bases, and can be counted on with regularity. Car bombers and petty thieves dog the roads like trolls under a fairytale bridge.

But everyone I met in Iraq seemed to feel he or she was doing something important for a country or profession badly in need of their know-how.

Plus, the money is nice. Um, except for the journalists.

The Least You Need to Know

- Contractors, nongovernmental agencies, news organizations, and the military have the jobs in Iraq.
- The money and benefits are often as good as you've heard.
- Networking can lead you to the best jobs and most reliable employers.
- Be ready for hardship if you plan to work in Iraq.

Chapter 4

Getting In

In This Chapter

- Traveling to and from Iraq
- The joys of booking unscheduled flights
- Getting your Iraqi visa
- Health concerns

Unless you vacation in war zones, deliver legal documents in Colombia, or have ice in your veins, flying into Iraq the first time will likely be nerve-wracking.

Your heart will be in your throat. When you land, confusion will reign. And when everything works, it'll leave you immensely self-satisfied. In this chapter, a look at the i's to dot and t's to cross.

Travel Information

Besides oil, tourism capitalizing on Iraq's history was once a mainstay of its economy. And like the oil industry, nothing travel related is stable yet.

The ancient ruins of Bablyon are on a military base. The Ziggarat of Ur is within a fortified camp. Lake Habbaniya, once a popular picnic site for Iraqis, has been a refugee camp for people displaced from Fallujah.

And in 2005, the head of Iraq's tourism board, Ahmed al-Jabouri, said he thinks a pleasure visit could well be a "one-way trip" for Westerners at the moment. "I advise them to be patient and wait for a short time," he says.

Nevertheless, ground is being broken for a 5-star, 28-floor hotel in Sulimaniyah in northern Iraq, and plans are afoot to return Iraq to its, ahem, historic tourism footing. When things get quieter.

Tour, Anyone?

Unbelievably, tour operator Hinterland Travel has begun scheduling trips to Iraq for 2005 and 2006—probably the only company to do so. If Baghdad and the South prove too difficult, operators vow to shift to northern Iraq and a tour of Kurdistan.

Inshallah, the tour will cost $2,257, which includes ground transport, airport transfers, site entrance fees, taxes, local guides, and hotel costs.

While budgeting for that dream historical excursion, keep in mind Hinterland's tour prices don't include extras—such as airfare to and from neighboring countries Syria and Jordan, where these tours have begun in the past.

Come Again

> **Inshallah,** Arabic for "if Allah wills it," carries the same sense as "maybe." In the Arab world, it's used every time a native speaker refers to something in the future. Blame it on ubiquitous uncertainty or pious humility, but it's the most common phrase spoken in any Arabic-speaking land. You'll get used to hearing it, *inshallah*.

Hinterland Travel can be reached at 12 The Enterdent, Godstone, Surrey, RH9 8EG, United Kingdom; Tel.: +44 1883 743 584; hinterland@btconnect.com; www.hinterlandtravel. com/iraq_upcoming.htm.

It just shows anything is possible in Iraq. But be sure *you're* convinced things are safe. From here out, you're responsible for your own safety at all times.

Time Difference

In addition to being at the crossroads of continents and global interests, Iraq is at the border of time zones.

It's three hours ahead of London (Greenwich mean time, or GMT), but jumps forward another hour (GMT +4) for daylight savings time between April 1 and Oct 1.

Keep in mind the countries next door have their own rules for keeping time:

- **Syria.** Always one hour behind Iraq
- **Jordan.** Theoretically GMT +2, but in practice on permanent daylight savings time of GMT +3
- **Iran.** GMT +3½ in the wintertime, GMT +4½ between March 21 and September 23
- **Kuwait, Saudi Arabia.** Always GMT +3
- **Turkey.** GMT +2 in winter and GMT +3 in summer

Public Holidays

With Saddam's regime gone, so are many national holidays. But Iraq recently added a new one: April 9, anniversary of the 2003 fall of the Baath regime.

As the new government gets established, we can probably expect some new holidays.

In the meantime, the usual secular and Muslim religious holidays remain:

- January 1, 2006—New Year's Day
- January 6—Army Day
- January 13—Eid al-Adha (Feast of the Sacrifice)
- January 31—Islamic New Year
- February 9—Ashoura
- April 9—Fall of Saddam

- April 11—Mouloud (Birth of the Prophet Muhammad)
- May 1—Labor Day
- July 14—National Day
- July 17—Republic Day
- August 8—Ceasefire Day (End of Iran-Iraq War)
- October 22–24—Eid al-Fitr (End of Ramadan)

In the lunar month of Ramadan, just before Eid al-Fitr, Muslims fast by day and feast at night. Normal business schedules become a shambles, and most eateries close for the day. Restrictions on smoking and drinking often pop up, too.

As for weekends, the Iraqi government has declared the normal work week as from Sunday through Thursday. Friday is the hard-and-fast day of rest. Still, some offices and businesses are open Saturday through Wednesday. When you need to get something done, every weekend can seem to stretch for three days. Other weeks, someone's in the office even on Fridays. Phone first.

Also keep in mind that Muslim festivals are timed to local sightings of the moon; the dates above are approximations and dates vary tremendously from year to year.

Show Me the Money

After the U.S.-led invasion in 2003, Iraq relied on American currency. Though the greenback is still pretty popular, Iraq officially uses the Iraqi dinar, 1,470 of which make up a U.S. dollar (as of October 2005).

Except on U.S. and British military bases, cash is the only form of payment accepted in Iraq at the moment. In a world where the power goes out every day and even governments are viewed skeptically, you can imagine how Iraqis view foreigners trying to buy something with a piece of plastic. They'll look at it like it's from the moon, then demand payment.

For big purchases, hotel bills, and office salaries, the U.S. dollar is still the common form of currency. It was once necessary to carry a supply of dollars and dinars with you as you entered the country. Now, it's possible to have funds transferred into Iraq through commercial banks, usually by making arrangements with satellite banks in Jordan or Kuwait. This is advisable even though it takes a couple of weeks to move the money back and forth. But it can be withdrawn in Iraq in cash dollars, a real benefit if you have to pay local employees.

Ask your colleagues which banks have the smoothest and most reliable procedures. If you must bring cash into the country, buy at least some of your Iraqi currency before entering the country. The exchange rate is usually better.

Papers, Please!

Of all the things I sweat before a trip to Iraq, getting my visa in a timely manner burns the most mental calories. Because the process has changed several times, it's always worth calling the nearest Iraqi embassy, a friend or colleague in country—or all of the above—to learn the latest preferred method.

Getting Permission

Whatever the current process, you must call the nearest Iraqi embassy to obtain a visa. There are several varieties to choose from depending on your purposes and how long you plan to remain in the country. You may want to obtain a visitor's visa, generally good for a month or less, a business visa good for a year, or a student visa. No visa is currently required for diplomats.

Lately, the Iraqi government has required foreigners to report to its visa office in Baghdad to negotiate long-term visas and to obtain an exit visa. The picture continues to evolve. In every case requiring a visa, you must have a passport valid for six months beyond the date you plan to leave Iraq. Check with the nearest Iraqi embassy, or with a professional travel document expediting service, what combination of official letters and photographs are required to obtain the visa you need.

As of 2005, visa processing can take three or four weeks. On your "to do" checklist, address this item early! See the Iraqi Ministry of Foreign Affairs website for updates: www.iraqmofa.net/index.aspx.

Numbers to many Iraqi embassies worldwide are listed here:

- **Australia.** 48 Culgoa Circuit, O'Mally Act 2606, Canberra; Tel. +61 2 62902993; Fax +61 2 62869952; cnbemb@iraqmofamail.net

- **Canada.** 215 McLeod Street, Ottawa, Ontario, Canada K2P OZ8; Tel. +1 613 236-9177; Fax +1 613 236-9641; otaemb@iraqmofamail.net

- **France.** 53, Rue de La Faisanderie 75116, Paris; Tel. +33 1 455 33 370; Fax +33 1 455 33 380; paremb@iraqmofamail.net

- **Jordan.** Between the first and second circles, Amman; Tel. +962 6 462 3176 or 462 3175; Fax +962 6 463 7328 or 461 9177; amaemb@iraqmofamail.net

- **Italy.** 355, Via Della Camilluccia 00135, Rome; Tel. +39 6 063 014 508; romemb@iraqmofamail.net

- **Turkey.** Gaziosman Pasa-Turan Emeksiz sok no.11, Ankara; Tel. +90 312 468 4834 or 468 7421; Fax +90 312 468 4832; ankemb@iraqmofamail.net

- **United Arab Emirates.** Tel. +971 4 268 5445; Fax +971 4 262 5242; dubemb@iraqmofamail.net

- **United Kingdom.** 169 Knightsbridge, London SW7 1DW; Tel. +44 20 7581 2264; Fax +44 20 7589 3356

- **United States.** 1801 P Street NW, Washington, D.C. 20036; Tel. +1 202 483-7500; Fax +1 202 462-5066

In addition to having a valid, up-to-date passport, it's also a good idea to keep a few photocopies of both passport and visa in your luggage and on your person. Just in case.

And heads-up: if your passport contains an Israeli visa stamp, it will probably be rejected by the Iraqi government. This is so common in Middle Eastern countries that the U.S. government allows its citizens to petition to hold a second passport. Always use the same one when you travel to Israel. Never use it when you travel to Muslim countries.

What to Bring

Besides the passport and visa, you need to bring some cash to Iraq. Where you go in Iraq—and how long you plan to stay there—will determine what else you bring. Men and women should have clothes that fully cover arms and legs, though men have more leeway with short-sleeved shirts in the summer. Because of the heat, cotton is the most comfortable fabric to wear. You can decide to dress like a Westerner, like the locals, or both as appropriate. At least in this respect, most things are available in Baghdad.

Have a dependable watch, an alarm clock, flashlight (with red lens for combat areas), electrical adapters if your appliances aren't British, and surge-stopping power strips to plug in and recharge your bigger equipment. (Local electrical supply is 220 volts, AC 50Hz.) Toiletries are in good supply, though women who won't be visiting Western military bases should bring a good supply of feminine products, as the local stuff is pretty basic.

It's a good idea to bring spare batteries for your small electronics, laptop, satellite phone, and cell phone. Landline telephones are spotty, and most Iraqis have cell phones. The local Baghdad carrier, Iraqna, has been reliable, but there have been recent problems, and you should check the section on cell phones in Chapter 5 before making a final decision. Satellite phones and/or international cell phones have also been popular.

Have a warm jacket for the winter season, bug repellant and suntan lotion for the hot days, and any medication your doctor advises. In addition to that, bring over-the-counter remedies for heartburn, diarrhea, athlete's foot, and minor cuts.

For women, there are three types of local dress: Western clothing; Western clothing with a scarf called a *hijab*; and the black, full-length *abaya*. You must have a scarf that covers all of your hair to visit a mosque, and an *abaya* to get into a Shia shrine. Customs are more lenient for men; but if you plan to mix with the locals, some facial hair is a good idea.

It remains an open question whether you should carry a weapon. If you are in the military or are an authorized contractor, this will be a moot point. NGOs are unarmed. So are journalists, though their local security people are a different story. Find out what your employer's expectations are about this very serious matter.

If your job involves working in combat areas, you should have a helmet, heavy ballistic vest capable of stopping bomb shrapnel, and ballistic shooting goggles like the ones made by Wiley-X. The latter are sold on military bases, but you can order them online ahead of time or buy them in gun shops stateside, too.

A final note on that: it's a bad idea to wear that stuff around the locals—even on the road—because it rudely implies you don't trust them and also marks you as a Western target.

Getting There

Just looking at a map of Iraq's central location, it would seem there were loads of ways to get into the country. Theoretically, that's true. In practice, every avenue carries risks of one sort or another.

The most common point of departure for Westerners is Amman, Jordan, with a number of hotels that also happen to be hubs for the latest advice on journeying into Iraq.

The perennial favorites include the plush and pricey Four Seasons (www.fourseasons.com/amman; Tel. +962 6 550 5555; from $212), Hotel Intercontinental (www.ichotelsgroup.com; +962 6 464 1361; from $162), and the thrifty and friendly Saraya Hotel (www.sarayahotel.com; Tel. +962 6 465 6791; from $22.)

But even here, on Nov. 9, 2005, groups of suicide bombers attacked Amman's Radisson SAS, Grand Hyatt and Days Inn hotels. Some 58 people, plus the three bombers, were killed, while 11 Jordanian officials resigned in the subsequent shakeup. Rules curbing the influx of foreigners have been likewise ratcheted up. Be aware of security risks in Amman—despite the sense of security you may feel there.

From Amman, your final options are to fly into Baghdad or drive there across the desert——a move that is distinctly inadvisable.

Flying into Iraq

Although Amman is the most popular jumping off point to Baghdad International Airport (BIAP), local carriers including Royal Jordanian, Kuwait Airways, and Iraqi Airways also fly between Baghdad, Kuwait City, and Damascus.

Royal Jordanian won't list its Amman flights to Baghdad online or with travel agents, but you can still get them—round trip and one way—at Queen Alia International Airport in Amman, +962 6 445 3333, through the RJ information office, +962 6 445 3200, or in the shopping arcade at the Hotel Interconti-nental Amman, near the third circle. Prices range from $515 one way to $1,115 round trip. RJ prefers cash, Visa, or MasterCard, in that order (www.rja.com.jo). Put your American Express away. I've tried.

Iraqi Airways is expanding service, and now has daily flights to Baghdad from Amman ($592 round trip) and from Damascus ($456 round trip). There's also reportedly round trip service from Dubai every day but Monday ($476), from Istanbul three times a week ($733 round trip), and from Beirut on Sun-days and Tuesdays ($700 round trip).

Phone first. In Baghdad, the Iraqi Airways ticket office is in the lobby of the Palestine Hotel. In London, you can get tickets from IKB Travel & Tours, www.ikbtravel.com, +44 20 7 724 8455.

Iraqi Airways also has a 24-hour reservation office in Dubai, United Arab Emirates, + 971 4 316 6666 or -6866. If you're in Dubai, you pick up the tickets at the Dnata Travel desk in Dubai International Airport. Take note: if you reserve the tickets outside the UAE or Iraq, you'll have to wire payment in U.S. dollars at least three days ahead of your flight, and will be charged an extra $100.

Flying Carpet Airways makes regular trips into Baghdad every Monday and Thursday morning from Beirut. They return to Beirut the same day. Fares are $500 one-way or $1,000 round trip. Tickets can be had through their agent in Beirut, Bassem Daouk, bisso747@hotmail.com.

And recently, an airline called Air Bravura has listed flights from Dubai to Baghdad for about $272, one way. They can be reached at +971 4 297 9490 (www.airbravura.com).

Iraqi Airways flights are on and off. Reliable information is hard to come by, but rumored to be coming soon are flights between Baghdad, Basra in the south, and Erbil in the north. *Inshallah*.

When transiting through Amman, there is a 10 Jordanian dinar fee for an entrance visa, and a 5 Jordanian dinar exit fee.

Landing in Baghdad is hair-raising. Here's what to expect: at 30,000 feet *directly* above the airport, the pilot will begin a stomach-wrenching, spiraling drop to fool would be anti-aircraft rocketeers. At the last moment, he or she pulls savagely on the wheel, and you will plunk to the ground, panting. Departure is the same, in reverse.

Driving into Iraq

Don't do it. Still, because the last air travel story might scare some off, I'll elaborate. The drive is currently far worse than the flight. The road from the airport to Baghdad is bad enough—often called the most dangerous road in the world. The road between Amman and Baghdad is similar, only it's 410 miles long, takes 11 hours to drive, and is fraught with the threat of attack.

Red Alert!

If you have to take this route in either direction, always go in a convoy with more experienced travelers. Spread expensive equipment and cash throughout the vehicle, and remember extra gas, water, food, and repair equipment. Be very clear with your travel companions about what you all will do in the event of attack or breakdown, and how you'll communicate in those situations. Don't stop or get separated along the way, and keep a sharp lookout for ambushes.

Along the way, highway piracy is commonplace, and kidnappings have been attempted near the very dangerous towns of Rutbah, Ramadi, and Fallujah in the Sunni heartland of Iraq's western Anbar province.

The road itself could be any interstate highway in the United States—two well-made lanes in each direction, though they're a little worse for wear from all the armored traffic they've seen.

This Just In

A note on bribery: officially, no one condones such a thing. But it can come up in Iraq, especially at entry points. You may have visa troubles, or someone may *find* "visa troubles." There may be questions with some of your electronic equipment—any number of pretexts can arise. You should resist pressure to pay a bribe, but sometimes there's no other choice. Keep in mind the fellow travelers behind you, and whatever you do, don't try bribery to smooth over actual illegal activity. Still, having a few extra $20 bills can come in handy, as does a carton of decent cigarettes, a steady smile, and a polite attitude.

To get to Baghdad from Jordan, most leave Amman in the middle of the night and pass the oddly bustling border point at Trebil, Iraq, at first light.

Passports are given to the passport control office, where you wait for your name to be called, pay a 5 Jordanian dinar exit fee, and go.

In the opposite direction, expect to wait for hours at the border, as poorly paid Iraqi customs officials—or imposters posing as officials—demand one bribe after another. Eventually, they'll stamp your passport, and you'll be on your way. Entry into Jordan requires a fee of 10 Jordanian dinars. It's hard to say what leaving Iraq by car will cost you.

Opinions differ, but flying is probably safer at this time.

Health

Sadly, modern medical care and medicines aren't widely available in Iraq. Many facilities aren't up and running at all, and medical supplies have been badly depleted everywhere. What remains usually fails to meet Western standards.

At the very least, information on vaccinations and other health precautions—such as food and water precautions and advice about insect bites—can be obtained from the Centers for Disease Control and Prevention's hotline for international travelers. You can reach them at +1 877 394-8747, Fax +1 888 232-3299, or via the CDC website at www.cdc.gov/travel.

Information on infectious disease outbreaks can be found on the World Health Organization website at www.who.int/en.

Among other peculiar maladies, the bite of infected
sand flies can give you leishmaniasis, a slowly
spreading, ulcerated scar with an occasionally life-
threatening fever. Infected dogs are carriers, and
the risk is higher outside Baghdad. (I can't tell
whether mine came from Kurdistan or the Syrian
border, but bug spray would have prevented it.)

Also, you should be aware that food reactions—and
I'm talking about diarrhea here—are very common.
Once you arrive in country, you should ask a few
fellow foreigners how they manage the problem. In
extreme cases, dehydration is a risk, and a trip to
the hospital may be necessary.

Before you leave, it's an overall good idea to go to
your local travel clinic or doctor for vaccinations
and other medical advice. In general, don't trust
the water, undercooked meat, or food handled in
unsanitary conditions. Ask your doctor about im-
munization for hepatitis A and B, tetanus, typhoid,
rabies, malaria, and the other nasty ailments
endemic to the area.

Weather

Bigger than California, Germany, or Japan, Iraq is
a giant of a place with mountains in the Kurdish
north, marshes in the Shiite south, and high desert
plateaus between.

The weather varies with location and time of year.
In Baghdad, temperatures range from average highs
in July around 110°F (43°C) to lows in January of

38°F (3°C). Elsewhere, temperatures pass 100°F (38°C) sometime in the late spring, then remain over 80°F (27°C) all summer, even at night. Humidity is usually pretty low—except around the rivers (where most people live), where it can get positively steamy. It's worse the farther south you go. Near the Persian Gulf, the summer heat index reaches more than 120°F (48°C).

Checking In

There is an entire chapter on personal security, but wherever you stay in Iraq it is advisable to check in with your country's nearest embassy or consulate as soon as possible. If your country doesn't have a consulate in Iraq, check in with officials from a country friendly to yours that does have a presence.

Citizens of the United States can find the nearest embassy or consulate through the U.S. State Department's travel registration website at travelregistration. state.gov.

You can also register with the embassy by e-mail (usconsulbaghdad@state.gov), telephone (+1 240 553-0584, ext. 5340 or 5635), or by calling their local cell phones at +964 7901 732 134, +964 7901 168 167, or +964 7901 168 383. The embassy is online at iraq.usembassy.gov and baghdad.usembassy.gov.

British citizens can reach their consulate by calling +964 7901 926 280 or +1 703 270 0254, by e-mail at britishconsulbaghdad@gtnet.gov.uk or online at www.britishembassy.gov.uk/iraq.

Australians in Iraq should register with their embassy through the Department of Foreign Affairs and Trade at www.orao.dfat.gov.au. For urgent help, call the 24-hour Consular Emergency Centre in Can-berra at +61 2 6261 3305. If you need to speak to a consular officer in Iraq, call mobile +1 914 360 3289 or fixed line +964 1 538 2100.

Checking in with friendly military commands is also a good idea. Units have quick reaction forces (QRFs) ready for emergencies, which includes responding to threats to Western civilians. It's not something I'd count on, but even out of courtesy, the military likes to know who's who and who's where. It seems fair to me. I keep on my person at all times the phone number of whichever com-mander of U.S. forces happens to oversee Baghdad. Military units will be happy to give you a contact number, too. The consulate or embassy can help you make contact.

For that matter, throughout your stay in Iraq, update colleagues and officials about where you plan to be as you're out during the day, and check in with them when you return.

Always Have a Plan

As a final word in this chapter, this advice: pay attention to details, and *always have a plan*. This will be a recurring theme in this book, as it should be during your time in Iraq.

Right now, this wonderful place is inherently dangerous. As in all such places, there will always be an element of unavoidable risk. Your job—and yours alone—is to recognize, minimize, and avoid all the avoidable risks.

There'll be more on this subject later, but please understand that neither this book nor any other can prepare you for all you may face.

The Least You Need to Know

- Plan ahead to get your Iraqi entrance visa.
- Iraq has its own currency now, the Iraqi dinar—best bought before entering the country.
- Knowledgeable officials, friends, and colleagues should be consulted throughout the planning stages of your trip.
- While near and in Iraq, stay in touch with your country's local consulate.
- Keep a list of phone numbers on hand at all times, and use them often.
- Always have a plan.

Chapter 5

Staying in Iraq

In This Chapter

- Settling in your new temporary home
- Life among Iraqis and foreigners
- Getting a phone and going online
- Hiring and firing

The new experiences begin as soon as you arrive in Iraq. You'll race from the airport through a bombed-out, trash-strewn city to strange accommodations that are home to a cast of characters like you've never imagined. There are Iraqis of every size, complexion, and disposition, American ex-soldiers working as highly paid contractors, a smattering of South Africans, the ubiquitous Australians, French journalists, old friends in a new setting—all of this in a place that will soon be your home, too.

On your first night, you'll be in the mood for a small celebration. Enjoy, but this is when you start asking the nitty-gritty questions!

Hello, Room Service?

It's unlikely you'll arrive on your own in Iraq, un-announced, seeking an unoccupied hotel room. Most of the bigger hotels have housed journalists, NGO workers, and contractors since Baghdad fell in April 2003, each passing the room to colleagues as though it was a hereditary fiefdom. Chances are, you'll be the next lord or lady of the manor. So here's what to expect.

You'll find the hotels have a patchwork atmosphere, and a décor more reminiscent of college dormitories than the high-priced accommodations they are ($85–$200 a night). But after you're situated, you'll come to appreciate the charm, convenience, and heightened security. As the insurgency ratcheted up, so did defenses around Iraq's major hotels. Blast walls, guard posts, sandbagged fortifications, and checkpoints are common—and should be expected.

Red Alert!

On Nov. 18, 2005, a twin suicide bombing targeted the Hamra Hotel, where many foreign journalists are housed, marking the first time the Western media have been collectively targeted. A few weeks earlier, the Sheraton and Palestine hotel complexes were attacked. All are still operating—but none should be assumed to be safe!

Here's a list of the best-known hotels by neighborhood, some of which keep unpublished phone numbers. Think of this section less as a guide on where to stay than a primer on what to expect when you get there.

Saadoun

This is the area of downtown Baghdad across from the fortified Green Zone, home to the largest hotels and contingents of the foreign press corps.

The Sheraton is the most famous (+964 1 816 0039 and -0093), on famous Firdos Square. It has sweet views from the rooms and rooftops, but is high profile, was recently targeted by suicide bombers in heavy trucks, and has been rocketed in the past. Security precautions nowadays are correspondingly high.

You Don't Say

Close by and benefiting from security arrangements for the Palestine and Sheraton is the Hotel al-Fanar, with its 40 rooms and cozy accommodations. It was the hotel of choice for Western peace activists and human shields camped out in Baghdad before the 2003 invasion. It also used to have a neurotic monkey and a parrot that could impersonate falling bombs.

Nearby is the Hotel Palestine (+964 1 747 0874 and -5678). Also a famous hotel for hacks, many news organizations are still based here. The rooms are spacious but bland, but the hotel houses a couple of restaurants and an outdoor barbeque. It's also been a past target for attack.

Karrada and Masbah

Karrada is Baghdad's beleaguered central business district, a bustling place next to impossible to cross at rush hour. Security at the hotels in Karrada and nearby Masbah is low compared to elsewhere, and many of the hotels seem to prefer locals to Westerners.

The Baghdad Tower Hotel has grand wooden furniture, tiny single rooms, and noisy double rooms overlooking the street outside. Suites in back overlook a pleasant residential neighborhood, and the ninth-floor restaurant overlooks everything— Baghdad is a sprawling city of mostly three-story buildings that peek between its ubiquitous palm trees. But again, security here has been questionable in the past.

Slightly more secure is the Rimal Hotel (+964 88 216 677 45 186). Guests here find brilliantly scoured rooms, a gym, and a sauna. When it's not closed, there's also an Arab casino on the roof—though it's more like a restaurant than Rick's Café in Casablanca. Make sure you and your more experienced security advisors are comfortable before moving in to any rooms in Karrada or Masbah.

Jadriyah

Jadriyah is one of the more expensive residential areas of Baghdad, and has become a popular place for foreigners who can afford it. (Despite Karrada's traffic gauntlet to reach the Green Zone!)

A recent bombing notwithstanding, the Hamra Hotel is on a well-guarded block a bit off the neighborhood's main drag, and has been correspondingly popular with journalists and foreign aid workers. Because the Australian Embassy used to be nearby, it also used to be at risk from falling insurgent rockets that overshot the embassy. But it has a nice pool, a decent restaurant, and decent security, which so far make it worth the risk.

Across the street is the Flowers Land Hotel, a smaller establishment with well-furnished rooms a little more expensive than they seem to be worth. Foreign aid workers congregate here, and it benefits from the Hamra's security. Also many news organizations keep homes nearby—so there's almost always a cocktail party to join.

Base, Sweet Base

Room service may not be on your desert horizon, however. And though guarded villas exist everywhere in Iraq, and are a possibility for some long-term visitors, most Western workers will live in barracks in central Baghdad's well-protected Green Zone, or on military bases scattered throughout the country.

If you're in the military, a contractor who works with the military, or a journalist who covers the military, your time in Iraq mostly will be spent within the confines of military encampments.

Thankfully, flush toilets, shower trailers, air conditioning—even satellite TV and Internet cafés— came to most U.S. bases between 2004 and 2005. It makes for a vastly different experience, I can assure you.

In future chapters, we discuss military transport between bases. For now, here's a sampling of the creature comforts you'll find inside the wire.

Cots and Cans

Depending on where you are, soldiers or Marines will direct you to a cot nestled in a tent, a bunk bed in an ornate room in one of Saddam's former palaces, or a plywood hootch. They could also hand you the key to your own sterile white metal trailer, variously called a can, a CHU (for container housing unit), or trailer. Hootches and cans generally have bunk beds with actual mattresses.

Dining Facilities and Other Facilities

After dropping your gear in your new quarters, you'll want to know where to eat. Gone is the quaint term *chow hall*, surrendered in favor of the much-less-colorful "dining facility"—or more frequently, d-fac.

But except for the most far-flung encampments, base d-facs are surprisingly pleasant places, run by contractors from Kellogg, Brown & Root, who provide tempting menus, lavish buffets, satellite television, canned soda, and Baskin-Robbins ice cream.

This Just In

A quick guide to the best dining facilities on U.S. bases in Iraq: the d-fac at Forward Operating Base Danger in Tikrit is spacious and enjoyable, but no comparison to the cappuccino stand in the main palace up the road—which offers espresso drinks and sells world-music CDs. The Marine Corps' dining arrangement in Al Qaim is outstanding. And there can't be a dining facility in all of Iraq to compare with Camp Victory's, near Baghdad International Airport. It has Asian buffets and short-order meals, all with a remarkable sports bar theme.

Because of the decent food on base, and few opportunities to exercise in the heat, you may have to guard against gaining weight—unless you spend most of your time on patrols eating brown-bagged MREs, for "Meals Ready to Eat." (Soldiers often complain the name is three lies for the price of one.)

House Hunting

Changing security demands in Baghdad have everything to do with your choice between a hotel or guarded house compound; but if you're going to be in Iraq for longer than a few weeks, you may think about renting a house. The amenities can make the country feel more like home, which in turn keeps you rested, more alert, and working better.

It should be noted, however, that this is extremely risky without heavy security precautions in place.

Chances are, your company, aid organization, or news agency has already thought this through, as well as hired a full staff of local employees. Should you or your organization be mulling the idea now, here are a few tips.

How Much?

Foreigners aren't allowed to own a house in Iraq, but they can rent, and real estate agents abound to cater to them. No strangers to the world of small business, Iraqis learned early on that Western companies were willing to shell out big bucks to lease secure homes in good neighborhoods.

Many contractors and large news organizations—especially the big newspapers—have houses in guarded compounds, either on blocked-off streets with other guarded villas, or within the security perimeter of a major hotel, or both.

The upshot for your pocketbook is that rents in Baghdad are expensive. In middle-class Baghdad neighborhoods like Karrada, you won't be able to find a house for less than $100,000 now—plus a $2,000 commission to the real estate agent. Talk to current home renters to get a feel for the market.

As long as your organization is willing to pay, make sure to spend it wisely—the extra money should get you a house that's secure, that's close to your support networks, and that has a trustworthy staff to run it for you while you're working.

Location, Location, Location

Where foreigners choose to rent homes in Baghdad tends to follow where they stayed while living in hotels. In the tense security environment of the past few years, the most desirable houses—those on blocks with upscale hotels—have been snapped up.

 Red Alert!

If you rent a house on a block with existing security, be prepared to chip in with overall security costs.

As you may have guessed, security is everything when it comes to renting a home in Baghdad. Before you move in, you should expect to have in place—or to quickly implement—workable security arrangements.

That includes guards and sandbagged fighting positions outside, clear film or tape on windows to prevent shattering after bomb blasts, a safe room with a heavy metal door in which to hide, protection against car bombs and armed assailants, clear avenues for escape, and redundant communications systems.

Have a Safety Net

Several private security firms based in the United States and Great Britain will be happy to advise you (for a reasonable fee) on how to pick and defend your new home. The same group often can also be retained to provide rescue services for you should you be attacked.

That firm will be the first layer of a safety net you should have in place throughout your stay in Iraq. It is worth the money to at least consult with them. (You can find a list of resources in the appendixes.)

Another element includes having a safe house where you can go if things get dicey at your primary residence. The usual fallbacks, in order, are an agreement with a nearby hotel, a colleague's well-guarded house, an Iraqi employee's home, and the Green Zone.

Establish those relationships before you need them. If you do need them, you can expect a lot of people will be anxious, heavily armed, and that time will be very short.

Communications

Cell phones, satellite phones, and Internet service form the backbone of communication inside and out of Iraq. Shipping companies such as DHL, FedEx, and UPS are picking up the slack for an otherwise dysfunctional mail system—albeit at exorbitant rates. Land-line telephones work, but only sometimes, and as of late 2005, questions remain about whether the current cell providers will continue in coming years.

Wireless communication holds the deepest fascination for Iraqis now. Under Saddam Hussein, cell phones and satellite television were outlawed to preserve his grip on Iraqi society. As soon as he was gone, of course, everyone had to have them. Right now, they work better than almost anything else in the country.

Cell Phones

Originally, Iraq's U.S.-authorized cellular licenses divided the country into three zones, with Iraqna covering Baghdad and central Iraq, Asiacell in northern Iraq, and Atheer in Iraq's south. Those limits were lifted in 2004 in an Iraqi version of deregulation.

Since then, Iraqna has had a hard time. Aside from rival Atheer moving into its turf, Iraqna's backup generators and cell towers have been attacked, and its service has grown spotty. But it's still probably your most reliable bet on arrival in Baghdad.

Can You Hear Me?

Where	Cell Provider
Baghdad, Central Iraq	Iraqna
Northern Iraq	Asiacell
Southern Iraq, Baghdad	Atheer
Suleimaniyah	Sanatel
Irbil	Korek

Lately, Iraqna service can be had for as little as $17.50, with calling cards as cheap as $10, and minute-to-minute rates between 6 and 12 cents a minute. You can also purchase international calling plans, which are surprisingly reliable. (I've used an Iraqna phone to reach family in the States when my satellite phone couldn't get a signal.) You, or more likely, an Iraqi colleague, can buy phone and calling packages at just about any Baghdad shop. You'll need to provide some sort of identification.

You'll also notice most American officials in Baghdad—and a few members of the Iraqi government—have cell phones that use New York's 914 area code. They're operated by American cell company MCI. If you're going to be working for either government in and around Baghdad, you may be able to finagle yourself one of these.

Internet Service

Major hotels have Internet service in their business centers, an option for the frugal foreign worker. But reliable DSL (for "dedicated second line") Internet connections can be purchased for your hotel room, home, or office, too.

Among the best known providers is Uruklink (www.uruklink.net), which offers 256-kbps home DSL connections for $270 a month, and more basic 64-kbps connections for $100 a month. Uruklink also has a less-expensive dialup service.

Like most Iraqis, you'll probably find yourself relying on Internet connections.

Hiring and Firing

Even the most shoestring foreign aid worker ends up needing to hire local help while in Iraq. The language is unique even within the Arab-speaking world. The streets are unmarked, dangerous, and crowded with motorists. And it's risky for Westerners to venture into the city, even to buy sundries needed to keep your newly rented house clean!

Hiring local help will help you focus on your job, navigate the culture, and remind yourself that you're a guest in another country.

This book can offer you guidelines about how to start looking. *Where* you start looking is within your own network of friends and colleagues in country. Ask around!

Finding a Translator

The first member of your local team will probably be your translator. Unless your organization already has one, your friends and colleagues in Iraq will be useful in recommending one.

Almost anybody, from any background, can make a good *mutajir*, so long as they have a nuanced vo-cabulary in your native tongue and can keep up with the pace of translation. But the best ones also explain cultural cues, the feel of the country, and how locals view the subject about which you're curious.

You can expect to pay anywhere between $20 and $100 a day for the best translators. Try to pick someone already known to those who work around you, and don't be afraid to switch translators often until you find someone you're comfortable with.

Come Again

Mutajir (moo-ta-JEER) is the Iraqi Arabic word for "translator." You're going to want one. One of the first Iraqi phrases I learned was *Wain mutajir?*—"Where's a translator?" A good one can save you a lot of wasted energy. A bad one wastes more of it.

Firing employees is a delicate notion. To make it easier, it's crucial to stress up front that every job is temporary (even if you don't mean it). Expect to pay some severance fee, but don't be afraid to refuse exorbitant demands for either salary or severence. Bargaining is part of the culture in everything involving money.

Wanted: Sane Driver

The next most important employee you'll want to have is a driver. Iraq's unmarked, winding roads are confusing enough. Add the traffic chaos since the 2003 invasion—and the very real threat of attack or kidnapping for foreigners—and you'll be glad to let someone else take the wheel.

Like all Middle Easterners, Iraqis approach driving with a wild abandon alarming to Westerners. They view traffic as something akin to a navigable flow of water than something to confine within traffic lanes. You'll want to find someone you feel safe with. And if you're uncomfortable with your driver, it's up to you to speak up.

Hire only with recommendations from others you trust, and don't be afraid to say, "No, thanks," if you don't feel comfortable after a day as their passenger.

Other Advice

A word of caution: be wary about hiring too many members of one family. You don't want to become somebody's family business, and their ties to each other will be deeper than their ties to you.

At the same time, your driver and translator may end up helping you find other reliable employees as you need them—backup drivers, security guards, housekeepers, or others depending on your work needs.

As with most things in Iraq, you're going to rely on your network of friends, colleagues, officials—and employees—to help you make informed decisions. Ask for recommendations and advice. Your network will be the key to making your stay in Iraq easier. Don't try to reinvent the wheel.

Always Have a Plan

It's impossible to anticipate everything, but try to think through common pitfalls before you encounter them. Talking to those who have been in Iraq longer than you have will identify issues you wouldn't think of otherwise. Use those stories as springboards for advice on what to do when something similar happens to you.

Know in your own mind how you plan to deal with staff joys (such as births), emergencies (such as injuries or deaths), or if friction grows between you.

Have backups in mind in case staff members quit or have to be fired. It makes a hard decision easier if you have to go through with it.

The Least You Need to Know

- In Baghdad, stay in a well-respected hotel with adequate security.
- On military bases, take advantage of the perks.
- Hiring local employees may be necessary, as could firing them.
- Seek advice from your network.

Chapter 6

Culture and Customs

In This Chapter

- Iraqi greetings
- Reading Iraqi body language
- Notes on family and society
- Definite do's and don'ts

Iraq is a modern country with ancient customs. In the countryside, where irrigation agriculture and tribal sheikhs still hold sway, it can feel positively feudal—despite modernization of electricity, water, satellite television, and cell phones. In the cities, there are urbane surroundings and Western attitudes, but changes are afoot, intertwined with the violence.

Though it would be confusing to explain how to behave in every circumstance, the best advice is to remember the most conservative customs, and ratchet back from there if your Iraqi host seems unconcerned with them. In this chapter, we explore some of the more notable Iraqi idiosyncrasies, a few cultural pitfalls, and the manners that will (hopefully) endear you to your hosts.

Greetings

It's romantic to recall that manners and customs in the Middle East have roots in the earliest days of human civilization. The offshoots of those customs are still found in modern practices and cultural mores, honed by centuries of desert living and tribal diplomacy.

Showing friendliness, generosity, and hospitality is a point of honor for many Middle Easterners. Buried deep in the Iraqi psyche is the desire to give strangers a warm reception, born from when nomads depended on each other for graciousness and hospitality to survive thirst, hunger, and attack.

Fine, And You?

Among the first cultural traits a Westerner will notice with Iraqis (and all Arabs) are the ritual phrases they use to greet you and each other. Iraqis expect to go through a whole gamut of greetings *every* time they meet.

Ancient customs govern these moments. To Western sensibilities, it sometimes feels like a time-waster, and you may wonder what could really have changed since yesterday. But keep talking—even if your replies don't precisely fit the questions, you're doing the right thing.

Red Alert! _____

Iraqi greetings are extensive, and essential: when someone walks into a room, throw out an *Allah bilk-hair*, meaning "God bless"; the response is the same. With the uniquely idiomatic *Iraqi Shaku-maku?* ("What's happening?"), the response is *Maku-shii, winta?* ("Not much, you?"). "How do you do?" is *Shlawn-ak?* (*Shlawn-ich?* to a woman, *Shlawn-koom?* to a group.) If you know the person well, ask *Shlawn al-ahal?* ("How's the family?") The response to any *shlawn* question is the stutter-sounding *HOM-dillalah*, literally, "By the grace of God," but meaning "just ducky."

Iraqi Sign Language

The Middle East has an entire world of communication by gesture, sadly lacking in Western culture.

Handshakes are common to both cultures, but the Middle East's lack the firmness of European and American grips. And whereas Westerners shake hands at first meeting, Iraqis find it important to clasp hands every time someone arrives or departs.

For that matter, Iraqi men are a lot more comfortable touching each other than are Western men. Hand holding, long handshakes, and grasped arms are common, as is less personal space. Contact between men and women is the next thing to obscene, however. And although Western women have a bit of leeway with handshaking, don't do this too often in public with male Iraqi colleagues.

What'd I Just Say?

Gesture	Meaning
Touching palm of right hand to chest after shaking hands	Respect
Tapping chin with thumb side of right fist, as in deep thought	Wisdom, Maturity
Bring fingertips and thumb together, fingers up, and shaking hand	Watch it, buster or Wait a second
Joining tips of *just* the right thumb, index, and middle finger and shaking	Adds emphasis to speech
Smacking the side of your own face with head slightly tilted, eyes wide	Surprise
The "okay" symbol of Western cultures	The evil eye
Quick snap of head backward, chin up	No or untrue
Both hands up, palms down, and simultaneously flicking middle fingers	Used to emphasize "That's no problem"

Eye contact between speakers is also important, and staring doesn't have the rude connotation it carries among Westerners. The exception, of course, is men staring at women. That's never good.

The Workday

Unless you work strictly with Westerners, work hours begin early in the morning and finish sometime in early-afternoon, the hottest part of the day. Sometimes, they resume in late afternoon and stretch into the evening. This is also when differences in Western and Middle Eastern culture are on starkest display. To avoid frustration, it's a good idea to keep a few things in mind.

Iraqi Standard Time

It's common in the Middle East for people to be as much as half an hour late for any appointment. If time is of the essence, you'll have to be polite, but very clear, with your Iraqi employees. Make no such demands for your business appointments.

Try to pad your schedule to allow for the proper flexibility. And also keep in mind the current difficulties in getting across town in a timely fashion. With the 2003 invasion, traffic laws went out the window. For much of the day, Baghdad is a solid clot of stalled cars.

This Just In _____

Don't make the mistake of barreling straight into shop talk when meeting with Iraqi colleagues. Arabs place high importance on maintaining friendship first, business second. Doing otherwise can be offensive. As one Kuwaiti friend explained to me, "Americans talk business first, and when it is done, talk about their personal life. For us, we must be friends *before* we do business!" Keep it in mind.

Men's Dress

Most Iraqis wear Western-style clothing, and Westerners should wear it while in Iraq, too. Still, it's advisable to blend in by buying fashions available or similar to those in Iraq.

The places to shop used to be the Karrada neighborhood and Arasat Street, Baghdad's affluent and fashionable shopping district. After 2003, Arasat Street in particular was flooded with civilian contactors, hacks, and aid workers pumping up the postwar economy.

No more. Threats, kidnappings, and assassinations of shop owners put an end to Western strolls through the shops and storefronts. To get clothes there now, you'll have to enlist the aid of an Iraqi friend. But it's still possible.

Throughout the Sunni portions of the country, you'll see Sunni Iraqis wearing traditional *dishdashas*, unique in the Arab world for their muted earth tones and hem just below the knee. Often, Sunnis wear red checkered *keffiyehs*, as well. Shiites tend to wear Western clothing.

As a side note: men don't wear shorts in Iraq, and you shouldn't, either.

Women's Dress

In keeping with the Arab sense of propriety, low-cut tops for women aren't acceptable, and although most of the country is pretty secular, longer skirts are a better idea than slacks or (gasp) short skirts.

It is up to you whether to wear a head scarf, called a *hijab*, in public. But you'll have to wear one that covers your hair (all of it) to visit a mosque, and a black, full-length *abaya* to get into a Shiite shrine.

Apparently, there isn't much concern with expressing your femininity underneath, however. On one flight from London to Dhaharan, Saudi Arabia—seemingly as we entered Saudi airspace—the attractive, couture-wearing women on the plane donned black *abayas* and transformed in a blink from runway models into people whose piety almost made them invisible. Stunning.

Modesty and chastity are important qualities for women in the Muslim world. Far from seeing it as a sign of being controlled by men, Arab women who subscribe to body covering see it as an act of faith, honor, and dignity. Among Iraqis, the *hijab* brings an aura of respect to the wearer.

Family Ties

As in the rest of the Arab world, big families are common in Iraq, and people are enormously proud of them. It's appropriate to ask someone you know how they and their families are doing. It's not appropriate to inquire too closely, however, unless you know the person well.

After an Iraqi knows you well, however, he or she will show a real interest in *your* family, especially in your children—existing, planned, or speculated upon. Arabs in general take considerable joy in their children, and Iraqis do in particular.

A pitfall for men is to be careful about inquiring too much about the female members of an Iraqi's family. Some families are more easygoing about this than others—but lads, it's best to keep this under close check, even if it does seem like harmless Western egalitarianism born of politeness.

Iraqi Society

After the 1991 Gulf War, Iraq's middle class was hit hard. As such, many of its proud citizens, including professionals, are now working menial or low-paying jobs to make ends meet for their families. They may end up working with or for you. Keep their past in mind.

The longer you're there, the more you'll notice among many Iraqis a grim acceptance of seemingly endless violence and political uncertainty. If a conversation turns to politics or the insurgency, you can expect them to have a strong opinion and to voice it.

Again, be polite, but don't be overly concerned if their opinion varies much from yours. The less sensitive the topic, the more you can feel free to argue. Iraqis enjoy a spirited discussion, particularly between men. As one old hand in Iraq joked, "The Iraqis are the trash-talkingest people in the world."

This can be true. Still, try to avoid getting *too* deeply into religion and politics.

Urban Iraq

In the years before the Iran-Iraq War, Iraqi society was moving quickly from ruralism to urbanity. As the country emerged into the global economy, growth in Iraqi cities—especially Baghdad and Basra—was notable.

The war with Iran only sped up urbanization in Baghdad and northern cities such as Mosul and Kirkuk. (Basra was a little too close to warring Iran to keep pace.) Out of this urbanization grew Iraq's once-strong middle class of merchants, craftsmen, shopkeepers, white-collar professionals, and civil service.

As people moved from countryside to capitol, they tended to settle together in neighborhoods that still bear their customs and ethnic stamp.

> **You Don't Say** _____
>
> Many homes in Baghdad bear a bright blue or white ceramic plaque with eyes drawn on it called the *Sabah Eiyoon*—literally "seven eyes." In a world where religion is often strict, this is a nice bit of superstition. The ornament is thought to bring blessings on the building and to repel envy.

Meanwhile, Saddam's move to brutally purge Kurdish guerrillas in the North wiped out whole swaths of towns in the country's mountainous regions. Residents there fled to Irbil, Suleimaniyah, and Dahuk, while Saddam stocked Mosul and Kirkuk with bused-in Arab families. Those dynamics remain unhappily in play; in Kirkuk, Kurds, Turkomen, and Arabs all vie for prominence.

Rural Iraq

Rural Iraq remains largely tribal in the area along the sleepy upper Tigris and Euphrates Rivers, as well as in the rugged tableland of the desert northwest.

In practice, it's the same as it has been since the decline of the Abbasid caliphate in the ninth and tenth centuries C.E. Alternately repressed and fostered by overseers, the power of tribal sheikhs endures in the countryside—though power is mostly brokered now through business deals, school funds, and connections to Baghdad, in addition to the traditional role of sheikh-as-mediator in local disputes.

Eating Together

You probably won't go hungry in Iraq given all the tasty food available. And if you're an honored guest in somebody's house, you'll find that meals are quite a production. (Cultural hint: if you're a guest at *all*, you're an *honored* guest.)

Before you eat, relax for a long conversation, breathe in the incense from the *mijmar*, and enjoy the offerings of sweet tea or coffee with pastries. Your hosts will continue to refill your cup until you insist you've had enough. (There's enough caffeine and sugar in those tiny cups to make your teeth chatter, by the way.)

Come Again

A *sha'lah al-bkhoor* in Arabic (or a *mijmar* in the Persian Gulf) is a tiny incense burner onto which live coals are placed in a bottom tray, beneath a bowl into which sweet-smelling sandalwood or other fragrant oil is dropped. Arabs and Iraqis are fond of perfumes, and if you're invited to an Iraqi home, you'll probably spot one in the living room.

At mealtime, enormous amounts of lamb, rice, and chicken will appear. As a polite person, you may try to wait for the most respected person in the room to eat first. But as a guest, you'll likely be expected to eat first. Your cue will be the eyes imploring you to take a bite.

Try the Lamb!

Thanks to the strong influences of neighboring Iran and Turkey, Iraq joins a handful of other Middle Eastern countries to lack a unique cuisine. Like the Iranians, they cook fruits with their beef and poultry. Like the Turks, they eat a great deal of rice, lamb, and yogurt.

Much else in Iraqi cuisine has roots in nomadic cookery. Desert tribes used easily transportable ingredients such as bread and dates—or ingredients such as sheep and camels that carried themselves. Later, Baghdad's central trading role in the Muslim world made it a hub for Eastern spices and Mediterranean flavors.

Although the style may be indistinct, there are some favorite dishes to look for. Masguuf is the traditional barbecued river fish cooked on skewers. Pasha is a slow-cooked mixture of sheep and other meats in a broth. A mixture of pickled vegetables called turshi is a popular side dish. Breakfast in Iraq is usually light—fresh fruit, or bread with cheese. In most of the Arab world, lunch is the main meal of the day, at which various hot meat dishes are served with rice, vegetables, and salads. On informal nights, dinner is often simple food such as sandwiches, though the steady Western presence in Iraq has given it a more substantial place in the daily dining calendar. Still, the menu will probably be exactly what you had for lunch.

Do's and Don'ts

While dining together or otherwise, there are a few simple things to remember so as not to offend your hosts. Among the simplest unconscious ways in which Westerners offend Iraqis is by inadvertently pointing the soles of their shoes at them as they stretch their legs or cross their feet. This is gravely offensive in the Middle East, as if you would walk on the person to whom the bottom of your feet are showing.

Likewise, guard against seeming like you're in a hurry among Arabs. Don't look at your watch during business appointments or social calls with Iraqis—it says you have little time to talk with them. (Come to think of it, we might take this lesson back with us to the Western world!) Time is rarely rigidly scheduled in the Middle East.

Pointing at someone or beckoning, either with your finger or a writing implement, is also considered rude. Only animals are treated this way.

And remember that hospitality is a big deal in the Middle East. You should avoid refusing anything offered to you, unless you can think of a tactful way out. The flip side of this can likewise be odd—when you offer to pay an Iraqi employee for his or her services, many will refuse at first, even though they desperately need it. Just play out the role until they accept the payment.

The Least You Need to Know

- Hospitality and routine are the key to Iraqi interactions.

- Don't appear to be in a hurry; time is rarely of the essence for Iraqis.

- Men should be guarded in their interaction with Iraqi women.

- Iraqi society has been badly hurt by wars since the Iran-Iraq War in the 1980s.

Chapter 7

Saving Your Own Life

In This Chapter

- This is the chapter you must read and re-read before leaving
- Planning your trips into dangerous territory
- Recognizing life-or-death risks from shootings, roadside bombs, incoming artillery, and kidnappers
- Developing self-sufficiency
- Common combat wounds

Let's not mince words: screwing up in Iraq will kill you and others. Learning how to plan for dangerous situations and to react well is the only responsible policy. No book can teach you what you need to know to travel safely in Iraq, and no amount of preparation will keep bad things from happening. In this dire climate, security experts teach not how to remain safe but how to minimize risks.

There are a number of specialty security consultants that offer one-week hands-on hostile environment training courses on these subjects. (They cost around $3,000.) The same firms also do in-country security assessments, as well as compile daily, comprehensive, and indispensable updates on Iraq's security situation. A list of those companies is included in the appendixes. Reaching out to them is strongly advised. A brief look at the subjects they commonly teach follows here.

This chapter introduces you to the concepts of cultivating *awareness*, figuring *probability* of risk, and planning *evasion* of risks when advisable. (We'll call it APE for short). This shorthand approach to decision making will help you save your own life.

Planning

Planning is essential, and one of the few ways in which you can minimize risk and practice control of your own fate. A sound plan should address what you want to accomplish, the likely hazards you will face, and what you and others will do when those hazards arise.

The goal is do what you need to do, while keeping yourself and your colleagues happy and healthy.

Simple is always better. Your first steps will be to determine exactly what you hope to gain from some foray, to list the dangers that could hinder you, and to decide how to achieve your goal with a minimum of exposure to those dangers.

> **This Just In** _____
>
> Planning doesn't stop when objectives are reached. You should plan before leaving safety, again on reaching your destination, and tweaked still more as you approach each task.

Before You Leave

Before setting foot out that door, do background research that answers the following questions:

- Where are you going, how will you get there, what recent threats have emerged there, or on the route to getting there? Or right outside your front door?

- Who is fighting in the area, why, and what threats are at their disposal?

- How will *friendly* forces likely react to your presence? What must be done to communicate with them, and what are the consequences of poor communication? Are there safe places along the route if there is an emergency?

- Whose help will you need? Who will do the talking? Who are you traveling with, what is their history, and could they be part of the problem? (Do they get into tight scrapes a lot? Are they tired? Will they manage well in a tight scrape...?)

- Are there weather, traffic, terrain, or disease risks? Will those things conspire to slow you down and put you at greater threat of attack?

Those questions identify the risks you face. The next step is deciding how to manage them.

If you are a civilian and have the luxury, remember that benefits in Iraq often don't stack up to the risks. When that's the case, don't go. If the benefit far outweighs the risk, or if you *must* perform some task because you're *not* a civilian, then you must decide the best way to avoid or minimize the worst.

Discuss with your colleagues and security professionals (you will *not* be going alone) how you'll address specific threats. A different route? A different time of day? More security or less? Markings on your car or not?

From the answers to these questions will come your security plan. Before leaving, everyone must agree to it and know the parts they'll play when trouble starts.

Plan B

As we all know, plans go awry. Often spectacularly. You must plan for that, too.

Among the plan-altering things to consider are: what will you do if communications fail? (The hoped-for answer: have a backup.) What if you or someone else is lost or separated? How will you tell someone that you're okay, but delayed?

Red Alert!

All of these worries and more happen with regularity in Iraq. Insurgents and kidnappers change tactics on a weekly basis. Beginning now, your plan should include contacting a professional security organization for training and advice if your employer hasn't already. Remember this simple rule: no security plan, no go.

Still bigger reasons for backup plans include: what if you are injured? What if you are kidnapped? What if the regime collapses? Work these out as soon as possible and as often as necessary with colleagues and security professionals.

Taking Care of Yourself

It goes without saying that you should make sure you're in good health, and stay that way. Visit a doctor and immunologist before arriving in Iraq, watch what you eat in-country, drink only bottled water, and drink alcohol minimally. (As tempting as it might be, Iraq is no place to overindulge in alcohol—or any other substance that alters your judgment!)

Put thorough planning into every decision you make. Likewise, you should also have all the assets you might need. Obtain and understand your medical and life insurance. Line up skilled and trustworthy

translators and assistants. Have a safe place to
which to retreat in emergencies.

Before journeys, study a map of where you're going,
but compare it also with a deep appreciation for the
conditions and realities of the territory—including
its terrain, delays, and problems. Make sure your
intelligence is up-to-date. Carry and know how to
use the right equipment for the tasks you face.

Make sure your car is in good working order, with
fluids at the proper levels. Have the tools and supplies to fix a flat, or an overheated radiator, or other
common car problems. (And have another way out.)

Carry and know how to use a combat first aid kit.

Medical Training

You're going to need true first aid training, and you
should be ready to confront traumatic injuries in
Iraq—be it from a car accident, a shooting, or an
explosion.

After you have first aid training, use this section to
aid your memory. If you're squeamish, relax. War
injuries are so unreal—and you'll be so busy—that
you won't notice your nerves until later.

Whatever happens, take a deep breath, keep calm,
and appraise the situation.

First: don't get hurt trying to help. Determine the
danger to yourself. Second: check to see if there is
a continuing danger to the victim. Third: if yes,

move the victim from the danger, or else move the danger away, if possible

Only then should you give medical assistance. As a last step, evacuate your patient and find more extensive medical assistance.

Primary Survey

When assessing how badly your patient is hurt, remember your ABCs. In this case, they stand for airway, breathing, circulation, and continue with disability, deformity, and exposure.

Checking them is called a "primary survey," and this is the order in which you assess, and then treat, a person's injuries.

This Just In _____

If there is more than one victim, you're going to have to decide who's hurt worst, then second-worst, who's got the lightest injuries, and so on. If they're unconscious, that's bad. If they're talking or screaming, it's not as bad. If they're trying to get your attention, they may be in the best shape of all. Remember to chill out, and use all the resources you have around you.

The primary survey is conducted in this order because a person cannot breathe with an obstructed airway. Without breathing, a brain quickly dies of oxygen starvation. Less urgently, but still in the big three, is "circulation." Without breathing or a pulse, oxygen cannot reach what it needs to reach; both rescue breathing and cardiopulmonary resuscitation will be needed if the person isn't breathing or doesn't have a pulse. (Learn how to do both.)

Obviously, and still under "circulation," a person with a bad wound can bleed to death. Use judgment to decide whether addressing the bleeding or giving CPR gets first priority. When there is any question of a trauma injury, cut away clothing around the suspected wound immediately. You need to see what you're working with.

Red Alert!

With traumatic combat injuries, the risk of catastrophic bleeding is likely to be great. Many combat first-aid kits now contain a coagulant called "Quick Clot," which chemically cauterizes severe arterial wounds—the gushing, life-ending kind. If you find yourself in that situation, don't bother with a primary survey, stem the arterial bleeding first! The victim's life depends on it.

This is all done in the span of a few seconds to a few minutes, and only experience or repetitious practical study with a certified medical instructor can help you.

Here are a few reminders:

- Breathing should not be noisy, and there should be 16 to 18 breaths a minute.
- A pulse of 60 to 80 beats per minute is ideal.
- For an adult, the ratio of CPR compressions to rescue breaths is 15 to 2.

If all is stable at this point, you're ready for the secondary survey. You should repeat the primary and secondary surveys every 15 minutes and record what you find. The information will help medics or doctors when you reach them.

Secondary Survey

The "secondary survey" comes after you have stabilized your patient between primary surveys, and are going back over to see what you missed. If something unseen happened in a car accident or explosion, it will reveal itself in the secondary survey. Do not give painkillers until after you've done all of this.

We pick up the alphabet with D and E. "Disability" refers to mental impairment (i.e., brain damage). Uneven pupil dilation and nonresponsiveness are the most common signs. You can't treat impairment, but you must note it. "Deformity" is just how it sounds— you're noting if the body is misshapen by injury and treating what you can, or must, until better care can be given.

Next you must consider "exposure" to the environment. If the patient is in danger of baking in the sun or freezing at night, you must take precautions to prevent it.

The last step is to check the patient's level of consciousness. The acronym to remember here is AVPU.

In increasing order of severity it refers to a patient who is *alert*, reacts to *vocal* interrogation, reacts to *pain* (by pinching, etc.), or else is *unconscious* and *unresponsive*. (I always thought of this as the "hey, HEY, *smack*, *shove*" test. The earlier they react, the better.)

Finally, give them a full top-to-bottom physical examination. Look at their ears, their eyes, into the mouth. Check the spine and shoulders.

Push lightly but firmly on the ribs, see if they wince or react when you check the abdomen. Push on their feet. Check their grip. Get a rough idea of blood pressure: normal systolic blood pressure is 100, plus the patient's age. (I'm 32; my systolic should be 132.) Diastolic (when the heart relaxes) should always be around 80.

You can check blood pressure with the thumbnail test: squeeze their thumb at the nail and it will go pale. Color should return in three seconds or less. The longer it takes, the lower the blood pressure. Note this and look for the cause. An internal wound? Something external you haven't found? Likewise, a pale or blue tinge to the lower lip means a person is in shock and not getting enough oxygen. (The body robs blood from extremities first.)

Once again, teaching first aid is beyond the scope of this book. The above can only give you a flavor for what must be done. Seek hostile environment training that includes a hands-on first-aid course for trauma—gunshots and puncture wounds, bad fractures, spinal injuries, severed limbs, bad burns, and so on. Singly and all at once. War is hell.

Awareness

Even when it's not a combat zone, life in Iraq is chaotic. Add gunfire and explosions, and it's a mess. When trouble starts, control goes out the window and life quickly becomes a matter of the odds.

Obviously, it's best not to lose control. But being in a scrape doesn't mean all is lost. In fact, if you're aware, thoughtful, and decisive, the odds are actually with you. Just don't push it. And have an understanding of the scenarios you'll have to face.

Car Accidents

You only have to see Baghdad traffic once to realize this is the biggest threat to your safety.

First of all, the roads are in terrible shape—when there are roads. Second, there is a certain fatalistic nonchalance to Middle Eastern driving that Westerners find unsettling. It seems to work for them, until it doesn't.

Don't be in that car. Make sure the cars you ride in are well maintained. And be on the lookout for a driver trying to impress you (his employer) with his high-speed prowess. Slow him down.

> **Come Again** _____
>
> If there is one Iraqi phrase to remember while being driven about, it is *"ala KEEF-uk bissa-YAH-kah."* It means "Take it easy with the driving." It works wonderfully.

If you're involved in a car accident, watch for serious fractures from high-speed contact between bones and car parts. Also watch for hidden trauma such as head and spinal injuries, internal injuries, and shock.

Hijackings and Roadblocks

Other violence in Iraq is sadly intentional. In areas around Baghdad, and sometimes in the city itself, insurgents in stolen police uniforms set up false checkpoints. They may demand cash, but they're also looking for Westerners and Iraqis they suspect are in cahoots with the American occupation.

Be wary when approaching haphazard roadblocks at road junctions, blind turns, or hilltops. Official roadblocks are generally well defended. If you see something that doesn't seem right, don't go up for a closer look. Turn around and drive away fast. You should know from your background work before leaving where the legitimate checkpoints are.

Expect shooting to begin, and plan to outrun the trouble. As soon as possible, report what happened to authorities.

The rules are exactly the opposite at American and legitimate Iraqi checkpoints. Never, *never*, speed up as you approach them. Follow all instructions. Have identification ready. You should do the talking, with a smile on your face. Remember that these are young people who are nervous and exposed. Behave accordingly.

Hijackings and kidnappings have occurred at private homes, outside of hotels, and in heavy traffic. You can prevent attacks in your car by varying the routes and times that you come and go from your home, hotel, or base gate. From then on, it is essential to remain alert.

You Don't Say

An attack on an Iraqi general's car outside Baghdad's International Zone (Green Zone) on Oct. 4, 2005, worked this way: the general's white Mercedes and his security detail in a Chevy trailblazer (two high-profile cars in Iraq!) approached the main checkpoint into the IZ. As they did, a dark blue car cut in front of the Mercedes, apparently to make a right turn at the intersection. The delay allowed a red Daewoo to cut between the Mercedes and the general's security car. The blue car sped off and the red car exploded. The suicide driver was the only one to die. Watch it at www.ogrish.com/archives/car_bombing_video_in_baghdad_4102005_Oct.

Mayhem on the roads begins in one of a few ways. Often you will notice a normally crowded street or road strangely absent of local pedestrians. An obstacle will be put in the road to stop you or slow you down. The obstacle may be a staged accident or bogus police. It is often another car cutting in front of your vehicle and slowing down. (The attackers are in a second car behind you.) Concentrated shooting may begin just ahead of you.

If you are able to execute a U-turn, do it immediately and speed away. If you cannot, do not stop. Never, ever, stop. Drive through the danger zone as fast as possible.

Kidnapping

The day after I first arrived in Baghdad in 2004, one of the foreign correspondents with whom I had dinner the night before was kidnapped. Within hours, he was allowed to escape, and he left the country before the day was over. His experience was harrowing and instructive.

His abductors told him they had observed his hotel and recorded his movements for at least three days. They chose to abduct him because he was lightly guarded and predictable. When he and his driver got to a busy intersection a block from the hotel, a dozen armed men appeared and pulled him from his car. The driver was helpless to stop them.

The economics of Iraq's kidnapping trade soon came to his rescue. The kidnappers were Shiite, and had no interest in him as a hostage. To them, his value came because several Sunni groups, including some insurgents, were paying good money for Western hostages. One such group, in fact, paid his "ransom."

But the Shiites released the correspondent before delivering him over when he convinced them that (a) He was not a spy, but a journalist, and (b) he seemed marked for death by the Sunni group, which may have troubled the kidnappers' consciences.

The lessons to draw from this are to be unpredictable in your travels, to have adequate security, a plan for escaping abduction attempts, and to work for your own release or escape in the critical first hours after your abduction. More on that in a moment, but suffice to say that case studies in Iraq underscore that the longer you wait, the slimmer grow your chances for escape. (Hostage-taking in Iraq seems to differ in this regard from other regions.)

Most important, it's critical that your absence is quickly noted by people who can try to help get you released. Good security people now have contacts in the Iraqi government and directly to local sheikhs and officials—to track you down, and to negotiate your freedom! Keep trusted colleagues appraised of your whereabouts and intentions, and keep in contact with them often. In the meantime, advice on how to behave in an abduction varies. Most experts urge that you not resist your abductors while they are on edge during this act. After that, the advice is to let them see you as a human being—and remember that they are, too. Be calm and inoffensive. Talk as much as they will let you. Seek commonalities.

If you find yourself in this unenviable predicament, keep thinking. Observe your surroundings. Use daylight, temperature, and street or house noise to tell time. Occupy yourself with chores. Observe when and by whom you are guarded, and make plans. Decide if the risks of trying to escape are worth the effort. And if rescuers appear, alert them to your presence by shouting—but don't aid them in rescuing you by fighting your captors. In the confusion, you may be mistaken for one of your abductors.

Mines and IEDs

The International Campaign to Ban Landmines calls Iraq "severely mine-affected," a legacy of internal fighting, the Iran-Iraq War, the first Gulf War, and the 2003 invasion.

There are statistics on at least 317 minefields, more than 1,100 leftover Coalition cluster-bomb strikes, and hundreds of sites where unexploded ordnance (meaning "bombs") are lying in precarious wait.

One of the goals of the U.S.-led occupation has been to reduce that threat, but there are still an estimated 8 to 12 million landmines throughout the country. The most common are white plastic platter-shaped anti-tank mines, usually stacked one atop the other, sometimes three-high. Look for the holes or disturbed spots in the pavement. The mines are stacked there, to direct the blast straight up into armored vehicles. Avoid those parts of the road!

While on foot, keep an eye out for green and brown plastic antipersonnel mines in the sand. Look for triangular red minefield warning signs, and for trip-wires. If you find yourself suddenly in a minefield, your first act should be to stop, calmly warn others (shouting *"MINES!"* works nicely), and then decide whether you can wait for help or if you should back-track *exactly* through your footprints to safety. It is advised to stay put and call for help—unless you are also being shot at.

If in a car, stop immediately. Crawl backward through the car, kick out the back window or trunk, and look for a mine below. If there is none, carefully step down and walk out *only* on the path made by your tire marks. In either case, remain calm, call for help, and report the location of the minefield.

It is reported that in western Anbar province, near the border with Syria, local insurgents are paid around U.S. $50 to plant mines in the roads. They have had gruesome success with American Marines stationed in the area, who now drive their Humvees and armored vehicles through the desert in some places, avoiding roads altogether.

Still, it is the improvised explosive device (IED)—earlier called a roadside bomb—which gets the most attention in Iraq. Insurgents early on stole tons of supplies from the former regime's massive, unguarded weapons depots. They lash 120 mm and 155 mm artillery shells together with fuses and, voilà, they've got a bomb. They plant them in roadside trash, dead animals, or under bridge overpasses. They use cell phones, pagers, or wires to detonate them. Some-times you can spot the wires. If so, drive away quickly.

> **This Just In** _____
>
> When traveling with the U.S. military, you should always wear a Kevlar helmet, a flak jacket with ceramic chest and back plates, and a pair of wrap-around ballistic shooting goggles. When IEDs and mines go off, sand and gravel flies everywhere; the goggles will keep it from tearing out your eyes. The vest and helmet will keep bigger chunks of torn metal from killing you. The military will insist you have and wear all of this gear while in their charge.

You must also be on the lookout for suicide car bombers. In U.S. military parlance, these are called VBIEDs—pronounced _VEE-bids_—for "vehicle-borne improvised explosive devices." Look for the seemingly empty car riding low. That's because it's packed with explosives. Avoid.

Riots

You should never walk into a crowd of people in Iraq. If you are a foreign aid worker or journalist who _must_ attend (or try to attend) a public demonstration, a detailed reconnaissance of the event and the area are essential beforehand. While you are there, you and your colleagues (you will _not_ be alone) must keep a close eye on the crowd's temperature so that it doesn't surprise you by becoming a riot. Leave before it does.

Before diving in, look for masked rioters, piles of bricks, or other weapons. If any are present, turn around. Locate organizers first, preferably by telephone, and arrange for their protection. Work the crowd from the edges, and monitor its emotional state. Have several escape routes at hand before committing to approaching the crowd. If things begin to change, leave immediately. If you're not 100 percent satisfied with your preparations, do *not* go in.

Incoming

The sound of gunfire is almost ubiquitous in Iraq, particularly in Baghdad. Firing machine guns into the air is a form of celebration in Iraq and other parts of the Middle East. It will unnerve you the first time you encounter it.

To protect yourself from intentional shooting, think about how you look to other people, particularly the nervous person with the gun 100 yards away. Are you dressed like an American soldier or contractor? Like a local the Americans are fighting? Dress according to the security threats of the day— that is to say, don't look like a threat to the armed people you'll likely encounter. This changes from place to place and depending on your objectives and personal preferences. Ask questions and make reasoned, case-by-case decisions.

Besides the pop of gunfire, bullets aimed at you make a crackling noise in the air as they pass, a thick *smack* noise as they hit a nearby wall or armor, or else that Hollywood *pchoing!* ricochet noise as they bounce off of things nearby.

Mortars coming in your direction make a dull "*boomph*" noise as they're launched, and a sudden, dull, "*BOOM*" as they land. They kick up dust. Incoming artillery rockets rush in with a "*scree…* CRACK" noise, and kick up a lot of dust. When you hear the first noise in either case, don't wait for the second noise before diving to the ground. Do it right away.

When someone is shooting at you, take immediate cover. Don't panic; you are at greater danger of being hit by a stray bullet or shell fragment than an aimed shot. But don't dally in the open. If you're not moving in a danger area, and solid cover is available, use it. Don't wait for the mortar to fall or shooting to start.

When choosing where to take cover, the best options (in order) are stacked sandbags, heavy stones, a concrete wall, bricks, and then cinderblocks. (Cinderblocks are shoddy cover in Iraq, truly.) Don't fool around behind bushes and trees. If you have to cower behind a car, cower behind the wheels and not the hollow doors. Brake drums are your friend! And don't pick the car rigged to explode—it's the one that's empty but riding mysteriously low, because the trunk or engine block is probably full of artillery shells.

When shooting starts, get down and take cover. Gauge your situation and how precarious it is. If necessary and possible, get to a better position.

Keeping Control

Back to the principle of APE—*awareness, probability,* and *evasion.* Every foray in Iraq is different, and you should try to keep as much control over your own safety as possible.

It is vital to understand what is happening around you at all times. Doing this involves:

- Being *aware* of and understanding actual threats, so you can …
- Assess the *probability* that those threats will arise and develop, allowing you to …
- *Evade* those risks to avoid becoming a victim.

Remember that fear is contagious, that people who are afraid make mistakes, and that keeping yourself under control improves everyone's chances. And, as many a U.S. State Department warning advises in dangerous countries: be alert to changing situations.

The Least You Need to Know

- You should take a hostile environment course before traveling to Iraq.
- The biggest threat to life and limb is a car accident.
- Remain alert to changing situations.
- If this chapter did not scare you into deep thought, read it again.

Chapter 8

Getting Around in Iraq

In This Chapter

- Choosing a mode of transportation
- Regional travel in Iraq
- Getting security updates
- Tips on avoiding trouble

As of this writing, Iraq is edging from a low-intensity conflict in the North and West toward civil war in the center of the country. Because of danger on the roads, particularly around major cities, the American idea of a "road trip" doesn't quite translate in modern Iraq.

It's unfortunate. Iraq is crisscrossed by an enviable road system that all but ignores Saudi Arabia but links Turkey, Kuwait, Syria, Iran, and Jordan—with Baghdad at the hub of the wheel. Ancient historical sites are scattered liberally throughout the country, including a few of the holiest places in Shiite Islam.

Before you set out, make sure you do your homework—including a hefty assessment of risks.

Build in plenty of flexibility for navigating danger, obstacles, and delays.

Got Wheels?

The trains run irregularly and are risky, regional air connections connect Baghdad with Basra in the South and Erbil in the North (but nothing in between), and the bus and taxi services aren't advisable. You'll need wheels. Gasoline costs next to nothing when bought from official gas stations—somewhere on the order of $.04 a liter. But for your driver, it involves waiting in line for two hours or more. This is how Iraq's poor buy their petrol. Rich people and drivers for Wes-terners buy gasoline from black market street vendors for $.20 a liter, although the price has recently skyrocketed to the exorbitant rate of $.63 a liter—about $2.37 a gallon—unheard of in the Gulf region.

Renting in Iraq

It's still possible for Iraqis to rent cars (not Westerners, though, for reasons of practicality). But it's much cheaper to hire a driver (see Chapter 5). The going rental rate for a car in Baghdad is $75 to $100 a day.

But for a driver *and* his car, you'll pay about $40 to $50, depending on the market at the time. This is much more advisable, given the aggressive driving conditions even on *normal* days in Iraq. Just be sure your driver is well vetted and recommended by someone you trust implicitly.

Renting Elsewhere

Rental agencies in neighboring countries hate when people take their rental cars into Iraq, for obvious reasons. Those who permit it insist you agree to a pricey insurance policy.

For this reason, those few who drive rental cars into Iraq (usually from Kuwait to Basra in Iraq's south) don't tell the rental agency where they're going. Let your conscience be your guide. You can find rental agencies at the airports or big hotels, (ahem) not that I've done it. Rates begin around $365 a day in costly Amman. Kuwait has been less expensive.

Baghdad—Hub, Sweet, Hub

If you're a civilian, you'll spend at least part of your time in Iraq in Baghdad, where international flights originate. The six-mile road between the city and Baghdad International Airport is often called "the most dangerous road in the world," and it's only partly hyperbole.

The BIAP road or "Route Irish," as it has been called by the military, cuts through the Firdos (Paradise) and middle-class Mansour neighborhoods. Insurgents have been staging car bomb and RPG attacks from there; it's not uncommon to see a thick plume of black smoke rising from the road. It's gotten better in late-2005, but is by no means thoroughly safe.

There have also been reports of trouble near the Dora Expressway Bridge on the southeast side of

Baghdad, as well as on the roads leading south from Baghdad.

But the biggest trouble area is around the International (Green) Zone in central Baghdad. Formerly Saddam's palace complex, it is now home to the new Iraqi government and U.S. occupation authorities. Checkpoints abound, and so does attempted violence.

Indirectly, security affects all travel in Baghdad. The July 14th Bridge between bustling Karrada and the International Zone is blocked off by Iraqi troops and police. That means the only ways to get between southern and northern Baghdad are to take the Qadisyah Bridge far to the West, or the bridges between Sadoun and Karkh far to the North.

It's only a couple miles. But the morning and midday traffic on Jamia, Sadoun, and Rashid Streets (often blocked off by construction or checkpoints) is bumper to bumper and interminable. Thousands of motorists veer off main roads and into neighborhood side streets, spreading the misery. Remember that attackers also use traffic jams to their advantage. Plan every foray through town carefully, and ensure you have adequate security.

Heading South

When you hear someone talking about the "Triangle of Death" (not to be confused with the overlapping "Sunni Triangle" that's mostly further north), they mean the area just south of Baghdad.

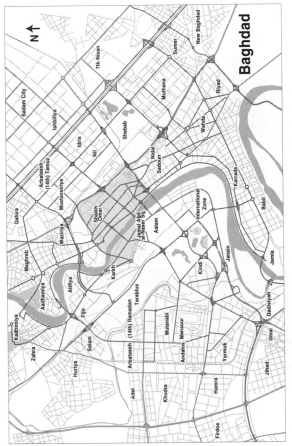

Street map of Baghdad.

Any way you figure Iraq's deadly geometry, this is an area to traverse only when you have to, only with great preparation, and only when you're feeling lucky.

The –iyahs of Death

Let's all turn to our maps of south central Iraq and follow Highways 8, 9, and 7 south out of Baghdad. Highways 8 and 9 toward Karbala have been particularly nettlesome. You have to drive them to get to the Shiite strongholds of Karbala, Hillah, Najaf, and Basra.

But to get there, you have to pass by Mahmudiyah, Iskandariyah, Yusufiyah, and all the other troubled "–iyahs" along the lower Euphrates.

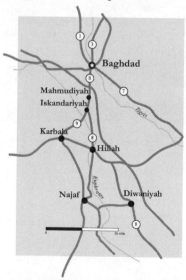

Baghdad and south.

Insurgent activity picked up sharply in this area after the November 2004 offensive in Fallujah, farther up the river. It's widely believed many of the baddies from that part of the world (see *Fallujah* later in this chapter) simply moved their operations south.

From here, they have used successful attacks and intimidation to hamper road travel between the Shiite south and the Sunni heartland in the center of Iraq. More recently, they have also seemed to be stoking sectarian violence between Sunnis and Shiites by carrying out targeted assassinations. Shiite militia have responded in kind.

Red Alert!

The area south of Baghdad is, for all intents and purposes, in a state of civil war, marked by roadside ambushes, IEDs, false checkpoints, kidnappings attempted and accomplished, and sectarian violence. If you can fly to Basra and more safely drive to your destination from there, do so.

It's not a good idea to stay overnight in this area; it's hard enough just trying to drive through it safely. If you must drive through the region, try to arrange to do so with coalition forces. And even then, polish your ballistic goggles and cinch your flak vest tight. Bad things happen suddenly.

Karbala and Hillah

The gold-leafed domes and minarets of Karbala can be seen for miles, heralding your approach to one of the holiest cities in Shiite Islam.

The city's three shrines commemorate Shiism's central figures Hussein, Abbas, and Hussein's cousin Owan. The mosque housing Hussein's shrine is said to be built on what had been the battlefield of Karbala.

This Just In

If you must travel south from Baghdad, consider taking a flight into Basra if logistics allow it. If you must drive, get the latest threat updates on the roads south, and information on developing threats where you're going. And travel in a convoy, if only because it gives a quick safety option in the event a car breaks down.

After you run the Route 9 gauntlet out of Baghdad, things are relatively calm in Karbala. Although episodic violence can erupt here on holy days (the crowds pose a tempting target), security in Karbala and Hillah has been calm compared to the rest of the region. But guard against complacency.

Najaf

When Saddam Hussein fell from power, pilgrims flocked to Najaf. Since firebrand Shiite cleric Muqtada al-Sadr and his Mahdi army militia holed up in its holiest shrine—prompting an American attack in August 2004—this holy city has been one of Iraq's loneliest. There are periodic car bombs and internecine Shiite violence, but it is one of the safer cities in Iraq. It is also the capital of the Shiite world, because the city is home to the shrine of the Imam Ali, son-in-law of the Prophet Mohammed. The cemetery nearby is among the most sacred to Shiites.

The gold-domed shrine is also surrounded by the once-picturesque alleyways of the Old City of Najaf, still in disrepair after the fighting in 2004. Pilgrimages have fallen by as much as 90 percent. Electrical and gas shortages rob the city of whatever remaining cheer it has had.

Nevertheless, this is the home of Iraq's Shiite Grand Ayatollah Ali al-Sistani, whose timely arrival brokered a cease-fire between al-Sadr and the Americans before the city was devastated. (Muqtada al-Sadr's reputation suffered more than the Americans' among the city's Shiite majority.) And the city's importance has been cemented in election after election in which Shiite cleric-packed parties have won the most seats in the constitutional assembly.

Basra

Things are peaceful enough in Basra that as of June 2005, Iraqi Airways has resumed air service to the city, making it an attractive base of operations if you must work in the South of Iraq.

However, the autumn of 2005 saw an uptick in violence between rival Shiite militias in Basra, as well as clashes with British occupation forces.

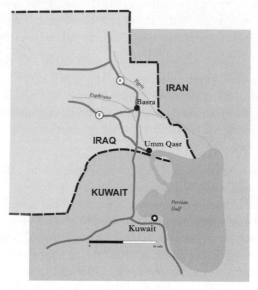

Basra and surroundings.

Basra and the nearby city of Umm Qasr down the Shatt al-Arab make up Iraq's only seagoing port. It's in one of the world's greatest date-producing regions, is a hub for oil refining and export, and is a place where temps of at least 104°F (40° Celsius) and wilting humidity are regular summer occurrences.

Because it *seems* far from the danger areas in central and northern Iraq, take extra precaution against complacency. In Basra and surrounding areas, a simmering feud is boiling to the surface. The players are leftover members of al-Sadr's Mahdi militia and affiliates of the Tehran-backed Badr Brigades, a militia associated with the Supreme Council for Islamic Revolution in Iraq, a Shiite political party. As of the December 2005 elections, it seems Shiite religious hardliners are gaining an upper hand here.

Efforts by British forces to quell eye-for-an-eye factional fighting have led to ill feelings for the Brits. Westerners, and British passport holders in particular should be aware of the possibility of being targets for retribution.

Going North

These days, you really get an appreciation for how diverse Iraq is by the differing motivations for violence when you travel. Unlike the sectarian violence in the South, the violence up north is more likely the product of disaffected Baathists (Tikrit was Saddam's home turf, after all) and Salafist Sunni fanatics nearer Mosul, each competing to outdo the other when it comes to disrupting the rise of a new Iraq.

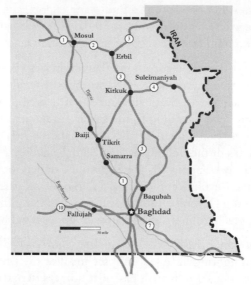

Baghdad and north.

There once was a time when driving to Baghdad from Turkey was a decent way to avoid the treacherous Amman-to-Baghdad highway. But now, the roads north out of Baghdad are just as sketchy as the roads south.

Since 2004, ambushes have been disappointingly regular on Highway 1 to Samarra and Tikrit, Highway 3 to Kirkuk, and Highway 4 to Baqubah. There have been shootings, roadside bombs, even car chases and shootouts.

Kurdistan

There is a bright spot, however, and that is the far-north Kurdish region everyone calls Kurdistan. The main cities are Erbil and Suleimaniyah. Though rival Kurdish political parties hail from each, they have benefited from a decade of protection under a United Nations no-fly zone, and are united as a power block in the new Iraqi government.

> **You Don't Say**
>
> Know your Kurds. The Kurdistan Democratic Party (KDP), based in Erbil and Dohuk has been led by Massoud Barzani since 1979, and controls the Kurdish Peshmerga militia that is slowly integrating into the Iraqi Army. The Patriotic Union of Kurdistan (PUK) was founded in 1975, is based in the mountain town of Suleimaniyah, and is headed by current Iraqi president, Jalal Talabani.

Kirkuk is another largely Kurdish city—increasingly so, to the dismay of its Arab and Turkoman residents. The current demographics of the city break down into almost exact 33 percent wedges, hampering local government even at the level of garbage collection.

Because of the ethnic divisions, there have been outbreaks of violence in the area, and the terror group Ansar al-Sunneh (the Sunni army) bases its operations here. The Sunni towns of Dibbis and Baiji have been especially problematic for Iraqi authorities and U.S. forces in the region, as has the highway, power, and oil corridor between Kirkuk and Baiji. Up-to-date information is essential before traveling in the area.

With great pride, Coalition forces announced in July 2005 that thrice-weekly civilian flights had begun between Baghdad and Hawler International Airport in Erbil. If possible, flying to Kurdistan is a much better option even than driving in a heavily armed convoy at the moment.

Mosul and Surrounds

Less secure is Iraq's northwest Ninevah province centered around Mosul. Neighboring Kurdistan's comparative peace might as well be a thousand miles away. Ninevah borders Syria, and foreign *Salafists* along with Sunni fundamentalists have clashed constantly with U.S. forces in Mosul and Tall Afar, farther west.

Come Again

Salafi is the Arabic word for predecessor, and refers to a Sunni religious fundamentalist. They're also commonly referred to as Wahabis.

The fighters have a strong willingness to fight and are growing increasingly interconnected with Baathist holdouts, who may in turn be supplying the money and technical advice to carry out the insurgency.

The insurgents in northern and western Iraq show a strong grasp of what is needed to target vital infrastructure such as oil and transport lines. They've been able to attack critical nodes, infiltrate government facilities, and snuff out government figures.

Westerners are also unpopular with them, and unprotected travel in these hotbeds of fighting is beyond foolish. Even well-protected civilian convoys must coordinate closely with U.S. military forces in this area. They are often edgy and may not take well to a surprise arrival.

Going West

Iraq's western province, Anbar, is big and empty, an area the size of South Carolina and then some, and mostly devoid of settlements. The exception is the Euphrates River corridor snaking in from into Syria.

The towns along that stretch of river have often seen heavier fighting than cities hammered in the 2003 invasion, which avoided this Sunni-controlled province. Progress in Anbar has been mired since, as it faces many of the troubles also seen farther north in Mosul and Tall Afar.

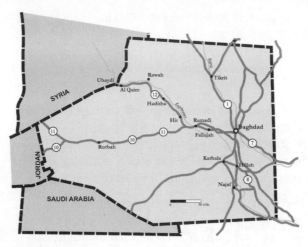

Baghdad and west.

The capital of al-Anbar is Ramadi. Until 2004, the capital of Iraq's Sunni insurgency had been in neighboring Fallujah. A pair of harrowing (trust me) invasions led by U.S. Marines mostly wrested the city from insurgent control. Ramadi remains troubled, however, and is the scene of deadly bombings and shootouts with disturbing regularity. Fallujah is somewhat better, but still incredibly dangerous.

The tiny towns north along the Euphrates—such as Hit, Baghdadi, Haditha, Rawah, Ubaydi, and Al Qaim—are worse, off the charts for risk to outsiders. In these clannish enclaves, even people from neighboring villages are called "foreigners."

Red Alert!

Hijackings, kidnappings, car bombings, and ambushes are staged with regularity west of Baghdad. In Fallujah, and likely elsewhere nearby, militants led by the Jordanian-born Abu Musab al-Zarqawi tortured and beheaded Iraqi and Western hostages. As of this writing, Zarqawi is head of al-Qaeda in Iraq, which coalesced during the American occupation of the country. Travel in this region is strongly discouraged.

The U.S. forces in this region are so overstretched they can barely maintain a presence in any one place for more than a week at a time. As of 2005, there were only a handful of Iraqi soldiers detailed to this deadly and deeply suspicious province. The border with Syria is wide open and scarcely patrolled; many newly built border patrol forts have lain in ashes since late 2003.

Highways 10 and 11 cross the desert through al-Anbar on their ways to Amman and Damascus. Foreign fighters are likely making their way into Iraq and Baghdad down Highway 12, the Euphrates River road.

You can anticipate snipers, suicide bombings, and ambushes in the populated areas nearer Ramadi and Fallujah. Kidnappings, IEDs, and suicide car bombings have been employed in Hit, Haditha, and

Rawah. Many of the roads nearer the smuggling town of Al Qaim at the Syrian border have been riddled with landmines thanks to local insurgents, who also double as gangsters. On the road to Jordan, there have been kidnappings, shootings, and intimidation tactics employed in Rutbah.

Unless you are in the military, a contractor working for the military, or a journalist embedded with the military, do not go here.

Embedding

In many cases, embedding with the military is the only way for journalists to visit portions of Iraq outside of Baghdad. (If you're in the military or a large aid organization, or work for a contractor, you'll have your own means for transportation. Otherwise, you're out of luck.)

Embedding is not a travel service; the terms involve spending several days to weeks with a single military unit. You live with them and travel as they do, sharing their risks all the way. Only specific and credible requests are taken seriously. Travel arrangements are never guaranteed, and almost always inconvenient. Make arrangements through the U.S. military's Combined Press Information Center (CPIC) in the International Zone, +1 703 270-0319, -0320, -0321, and -0299. Be aware that the numbers change frequently. It's always a good idea to ask colleagues currently in country which number reaches the most helpful person. The typical means for travel from Baghdad is by air, usually

a helicopter out of the International Zone or Baghdad International Airport. These jolting flights will
hopscotch you from one military base to another at
all hours of the day and night. Regional transport
out in the countryside is usually by convoy.

As a general rule in a convoy, try to get a seat in
more heavily armored vehicles. Don't ride in a
Humvee when you can ride in an armored personnel carrier. In an area that is heavily mined (such as
western al-Anbar), the seemingly exposed bench
seating of a 7½-ton truck is your best bet—it gets
you high enough off the roadway that the mine
blast is diminished by the time it reaches you. Guard
against flying debris with ballistic goggles, helmet,
and flak vest.

Always Have a Plan

The dangers of travel in Iraq make it absolutely
essential that you carefully and thoroughly consider
any movement in and around the country.

Using this chapter and the last one (Chapter 7) as a
starting point, you must assess your need for moving to another location and the probability of risks
associated with travel. You must then look for the
best way to evade danger areas.

You are the only one responsible for your safety
while in Iraq.

The Least You Need to Know

- Security concerns affect everything having to do with travel in Iraq.
- Highway attacks are common on the outskirts of Baghdad.
- Regional issues can explode into travel risks anywhere.

Chapter 9

Enjoying Yourself

In This Chapter

- Bettering yourself through exposure to history
- Exposing yourself to what passes for Baghdad nightlife
- Catching a movie in Iraq
- Party at your place

While in Iraq, you'll be eager for things you can do to pass the time pleasantly. And by now you won't be surprised to learn that pulling it off takes extra care.

Depending on conditions and your planning skills, you may be able to accomplish a visit to an historical site or one of Baghdad's many splendid museums.

If not, pop some popcorn! There are always Iraq's ubiquitous pirated DVDs, which are often first-run films. The other choice is throwing a party. It's between those last two options that most Westerners seem to spend their free time in Iraq—when there is any.

The Cradle of Civilization and All That

As described in Chapter 1, what is now Iraq has had a rich and varied history—both as the cradle of civilization, and as a crossroads between them. Baghdad in particular is home to more than a dozen museums that are crucial repositories to world history.

What is also astonishing to consider is that despite the area's long human habitation, archaeological sites continue to be uncovered, and in many cases exploited. In your travels, you may find yourself face to face with Iraq's heritage, be it officially conserved or illicitly offered.

Visiting Museums

If you make an effort to see Iraq's cultural wonders, find a way to consult with its guardians ahead of time to assess security risks. Likewise, take care to blend in as much as possible while out and about, and remain alert at all times.

There have been no attacks on sightseers in postwar Baghdad (probably because there aren't many sightseers right now!), but archaeological tourists have been targets elsewhere in the Middle East in the recent past.

In all likelihood, if you pop in for a visit at an Iraqi museum, it will be something you manage because it dovetails with your official duties. It's worth doing, but keep a weather eye for trouble and have escape routes in mind ahead of time.

You Don't Say

In the days after the U.S.-led invasion, Baghdad museums were plundered for their priceless antiquities. Some of the pieces were recovered and returned; others remain floating on the black market. Since then, the Iraq National Museum has gotten support from the United Nations to record electronically its collections for purposes of documentation, research, and preservation. The goal is to make the research available online for scholars and the curious. Electronic transcription of the museum's ledgers began in September 2005. Regional museums in Iraq may be next.

Below are contacts for some major museums in Baghdad. There are wonderful museums in other Iraqi cities, but the ebb and flow of risks there make visits unlikely. (Security in Baghdad is dodgy, but at least it's consistent, making it easier to plan.)

- **Abbasid Palace Museum.** +964 1 416 4950; decorative art, Arab antiquities, models of Islamic monumental buildings in Iraq; Abbasid Palace, Baghdad

- **Aqar-Quf Museum.** +964 1 511 1171; Baghdad

- **Baghdad Museum.** +964 1 416 5317; anthropology and ethnology, costumes, displays of local popular culture, and relics of King Faisal I; Sahat Al-Risafi, Baghdad

- **Children's Museum.** +964 1 887 9687; Baghdad
- **Iraq National Museum.** +964 1 361 215; archaeology, history of Mesopotamia; Karkh Museum Square, Baghdad
- **Iraq Natural History Research Centre and Museum.** +964 1 416 5790; Bab Al-Muadham, Baghdad
- **Mustansiriya College Collections History Museum.** +964 1 888 5765; restored version of the oldest Islamic college in the world, circa 1200s C.E.; decorative arts, archaeology, Arabic calligraphy, historical maps; Ma'moun Street, Baghdad

Archaeological Sites

With limited funding and spotty enforcement, Iraq's archaeological sites have been so plundered by looters that the whole country has been listed as an endangered cultural site. The World Monuments Fund says the ancient Assyrian capital of Ninevah, the ziggurat at Ur, the temples of Babylon and the spiral minaret at Samarra have all been impacted by years of conflict.

Pillaging in the south of the country is said to be so extensive that new digging sites—all of them illicit—look like a growing rash to passing satellites. Once dug up, these artifacts are smuggled away to neighboring Jordan, Lebanon, and Turkey, from there to be sold in Europe and the United

States. Some wind up on eBay. Others are sold as knickknacks to American soldiers. More than a thousand artifacts have been confiscated so far. If you spot something for sale cheap that looks like an authentic antiquity—you may, unfortunately, be right.

Nightlife

Few things in the world are more pleasant than an Iraqi evening in late spring or early autumn. If it were anyplace else in the Arab world, and you were so inclined, it would be a perfect time to pass the hours in a pleasant public place, people-watching and savoring a nice glass of tea.

This would be a mistake in Iraq.

Before the insurgency began heating up in the spring of 2004, there was the National Theatre (still functioning, but no one goes). There was the al-Ulwiya Club for families near the Sheraton. (It may be open during your stay; call first, but don't stay longer than an hour, and don't stay later than 10 P.M.) Nabil's, a favorite restaurant of Westerners, was hit by a car bomb.

Prior to the 2003 invasion, you could go to Abu Nawas Street for Baghdad's much loved fish dish, *masgouf*, and pleasant river breezes in the evening. As well, the restaurant stalls on the Arasat al-Hindiyah in Karrada might as well be a thousand miles away for as inadvisable it is for strangers to visit them now. Even the delightful kebab restaurant in Fallujah— once a realistic lunch destination—was bombed by the Americans.

I mention these pastimes-no-more only because your Iraqi hosts may recall them wistfully. It's possible they've found alternatives worth investigation. But security concerns regrettably trump most of the best options.

Besides, there's an 11 P.M. curfew in Iraq as of this writing, and most Iraqis stay indoors these days, anyway.

The Thrill of Watching DVDs

What's left for you is pretty much watching movies at home. The best collection of DVDs, cassettes, and music CDs can be purchased in the Karrada neighborhood of Baghdad, though it's best to give money to an Iraqi colleague to do it. You can also purchase legitimate DVDs on any American military base—provided you like action movies.

Pirated movies are everywhere in Iraq. These are usually the product of an entrepreneur who set up a video camera in a movie house somewhere. For $5, you can buy discs with two to three movies apiece, slipped into a cheap cellophane sleeve.

If you're in Baghdad, these can be found in the open-air looters' market at Baab al-Sharji. Westerners should *definitely* avoid this place; you can also buy insurgent videos of recent attacks and beheadings there. If you're in a military camp, the pirated movies are found in the local Iraqi shop that every base seems to have. They're notorious for crashing all the time, but for the price, it's worth the gamble.

Your Reading List

Besides bringing your favorite tunes and a couple indispensable movies, lugging a few good books into Iraq is always worth the effort. You won't be able to find many after you arrive. What exists are donated collections on military bases.

> **This Just In**
>
> It's not a bad idea to get a reliable, reasonably priced digital camera.
> While not on a reading list, those pictures are going to be something you want to see over and over again.

There are some surprising finds, but mostly we're talking about thrillers, mysteries, Westerns, and romance novels. That may sound appealing, but after a couple of months, you'll be kicking yourself for not planning ahead. I've often thought Iraq would be the perfect place to finish reading the great works of Western literature. In reality, you could probably cover quite a few regions!

Party On

Given the dearth of other things to do, the art of staying in and socializing with friends and colleagues has enjoyed a renaissance among Westerners in Baghdad.

You'll quickly come to appreciate good and gracious hosts, and will probably be called upon to host a gathering yourself—even if "home" for you is a hotel room.

The Civilian Host

In addition to the normal niceties of throwing a party are the added concerns of security in Iraq. If your home is not in a secure compound, or if guests will be traveling from outside of it, there is the very real chance that word of your gathering will get out to the wrong people. Avoid this at all costs.

For security reasons, many hosts limit their guest lists to immediate neighbors, and inform Iraqi workers in their hotel or home only at the last minute, if at all. This last rule is designed to keep word from reaching insurgents or kidnappers who might try to crash the party. In general, keep things as low-key as possible.

It is imperative, however, to let security workers know that additional people will be coming over shortly before they arrive. Guards are understandably edgy people, and providing a guest list is a good idea. With one particularly scraggly friend, I also provided armed guards with a description. The conversation went like this:

"If you see a shifty man with a scraggly beard coming over, don't shoot. He's just a journalist."

"*Don't* shoot?"

"No, not tonight."

Strictly speaking, alcohol is forbidden by Islamic law, though Iraq's recent past has been largely secular. Still, the country is growing increasingly religious. You should be prepared to make adjustments. If you're in Baghdad and interested in serving beer, wine, or spirits, you can still purchase them at the liquor stores in Karrada, but there are fewer and fewer shops left after threats and killings of shopkeepers at the hands of extremists.

The Military Host

If you're living on a U.S. military base, you'll be toasting with soft drinks or coffee. But other steps in your party planning will be greatly simplified.

The base PX (for Personnel Exchange) makes it much easier to do your own shopping. But you'll have to make do with nonalcoholic near-beer. On the other hand, gadgetry abounds on the modern military base. Television sets, MP3 and CD players, and DVD machines are frequently inherited from departing units, and can be had tax-free at the PX. Now *that's* one-stop shopping.

As far as where to host your gathering, you may decide your own accommodations are too small. Still, just about any common area will do for most circumstances. The post Morale, Welfare, and Recreation center may be an option for large, special events. At the other extreme, you may be invited to movie night in the Tactical Operations Center during a quiet spell.

Always Have a Plan

Even when making time to socialize—perhaps *especially* then—be sure to think through what to do if emergencies suddenly erupt.

Ideally, the planning process will prevent the worst problems. But it is a rule of thumb that when trouble breaks out, it will do so at the most inopportune moment.

The Least You Need to Know

- Visiting museums or historical sites is unlikely, but not impossible.
- Having a DVD and music player can preserve mental health.
- Extra foresight must be applied to social gatherings.
- Remain alert to your surroundings.

Chapter 10

The Hotel California

In This Chapter

- Getting out of Iraq
- What you'll discover on reaching safety
- Being burned out
- Redefining "normal"

By the time you leave Iraq, you will be obsessed with leaving Iraq. You'll notice time passing—your last Monday in Iraq, for instance. Your last 24 hours. Your last trip to the airport.

During this time, you could be on edge, hyper-alert to something going wrong. As you race down the road to Baghdad International Airport, you'll look for danger behind every stunted palm tree and broken-down car. Your feelings of joy and dread will be mixed with guilt at leaving colleagues behind.

And soon after that, you'll find yourself marveling at how detached the rest of Western society (*your* society!) is from the war where you just dedicated a chunk of your life. Should those wonderments morph into frustration and irritability, as it does with one in every eight other people who spend time in Iraq, you'll need to think about counseling.

Leaving Iraq

Just as getting into Iraq is difficult, leaving the country is no picnic. The process is easy, the chief difficulty is mostly in running the gauntlet to the airport.

But after the usual bureaucracy and confusion in the terminal, you'll suddenly be flying away. At that point, the real mental adjustments begin.

BIAP, Baby

For civilians, the trip out of Iraq is simple to arrange. If you're in the military, or a contractor working for the military, it's even simpler—follow the crowd. (Unless you're the poor sap who has to organize the crowd!)

Your credit card number and a phone call to the airline are enough to secure a seat on a flight out. Iraqi Airways can be reached at +964 1 886-3999. Royal Jordanian's office in Iraq is at the Baghdad Convention Center, +1 703 270-0167, or their office in the Baghdad Royal Meridien Hotel, +1 914 360-3362. You pick up the ticket at the airport, where you'll also sign the credit card slip or pay cash.

The road to Baghdad International Airport (BIAP) remains the Achilles' heel of the departure process. Check the latest security information as you make your travel plans.

This Just In _____

Though the final stretch of the road to
Baghdad International Airport is
unavoidable, you may be able to
lessen your exposure to attacks by carefully choosing a route down neighborhood
side streets until the last entrance ramp
onto it. If you come and go often from the
airport, be sure to vary your routes!

Your driver will only be able to bring you as far as
the first checkpoint at the airport, an interminable
wait in bumper-to-bumper traffic on the most dangerous road in the world. After you've been
dropped off behind the security gate, you'll have to
board a bus or taxi to the airport terminal itself,
about two miles away. The bus is free. The taxi,
which used to be about $5, now will cost you as
much as $12. They only travel on the airport prop-
erty. When you arrive at the terminal, you'll be
assaulted by baggage handlers, who'll want 7,000
Iraqi dinars or so (about $5) to carry your bags 50
yards. If you don't want their help, say "*la, shukran*"—
that's "no, thank you"—and say it clearly and force-
fully. They're all smiles up front, but all business at
the security x-ray machine.

You must pay for the ticket before passing through
security. The Royal Jordanian office is just inside
the doors, to your right, although sometimes you
have to go through security to pay if no one is at

the office. You must also pay a departure tax of 4,500 Iraqi dinars (about $3) when you check your bags (they accept U.S. dollars, but pretend not to have change for a $5). You may also have to pay a fee for carrying extra weight. This will probably send you back through the security line with your bags. Build in plenty of time. Resist the urge to become frustrated.

> **You Don't Say** _____
>
> As Iraq gets back on its feet, the government is increasingly strict about trafficking in historical items. This impacts you if you're carrying antiques or historical souvenirs in your luggage. The BIAP security staff will rifle through them, and in many cases confiscate antiques as "lost state treasures" unless you have the right papers.

Your final hours waiting to leave Iraq will be marked by confusion and delay. Generally, your departure gate is not announced until the last minute, and the flight almost always leaves late—sometimes by an hour or more.

Clocks tick; people shift back and forth in BIAP's uncomfortable college dorm couches and make several passes through the airport's unappealing duty-free shop. I've counted the sculpted pipes in the ceiling chandelier (I forget how many, thankfully), and a large mortar round once fell while I was waiting to fly to Amman. The ceiling sculpture shook, and there was an uncomfortable silence before conversations began again. The flight took off on time. Stuck between worlds like that, it's very weird.

Your last view of Iraq will be through the windows of the bus that races your plane on the tarmac. It is a boring, industrial vision. Things get more interesting as you take off, however, as the pilots (usually former South African military types) crank the engines to full throttle and pull up into a merciless corkscrew. You'll be pinned to the bulkhead or the broad-shouldered contractor next to you until you reach 30,000 feet. Then the wings will level out, there'll be a *ding!* in the cabin, and a flight attendant will push a trolley full of dry sandwiches and orange juice cups up the aisle. The passengers let out a collective sigh at this point.

Arriving in Amman

Though other Arab-world airlines are considering flights to and from Baghdad, your first stop after leaving the Iraqi capital will probably be Amman. You've never seen hills so pretty as the orchard-covered mounds around the capital of Jordan, especially after leaving frenzied, dangerous Iraq.

You'll again ride a bus to the terminal. You exchange money at the kiosk on your left before reaching customs, and then pay your 10 Jordanian dinars ($15) for an entry visa. Your bags will arrive downstairs, where you'll again run the gauntlet of baggage handlers (5JD, $7.50). Outside, you'll find the official airport taxis, where you'll pay 20 JD ($30, tip included) for a ride to your hotel in Amman.

Plan to spend a day or two unwinding in this middle ground. Swim, order room service, get a massage. You'll undoubtedly be eager to continue on to your home, wherever it is. Resist the urge if you can afford to. You'll thank yourself for the quiet day or two before the pressures of home.

What You'll Suddenly Notice in the Real World

By the time you find yourself in a Western city again, be it Paris, London, Zurich, or New York, you'll notice a few things about your fellow Westerners.

Specifically, although they may know that *something's* going on Iraq, they won't seem to know enough about *what's* going on in Iraq. The fact that you have just spent a good deal of time in Iraq will fascinate them. They'll probably ask you what it's *really* like, and then cut off your explanation by telling you what *they* think it's really like. (I've had this happen both with people who consider themselves pro-U.S. involvement and anti-U.S. involvement. None of them had it quite right, and talking to all of them was a little disheartening. But hey, we go so they don't have to.)

Finally, if you are returning to a job, marriage, or parenthood, you will be expected to step in and fulfill your role immediately. This will drive you crazy, and you will discover that …

You Are a Basket Case

This is normal. Do not panic.

You'll notice crowds. You'll notice unobservant people. You'll notice cars driving past you slowly. All of these things will bother you in someplace ill-defined deep inside. All of these things are harmless. And you may suddenly notice yourself saying that to yourself—hopefully not out loud. "This is harmless," you'll think, struck by the notion that *anything* could be harmless. You won't be convinced at first, but noting these changes is part of the adjustment process.

As for the people, it's not that they're naïve, or cruel, it's just that they can't possibly understand what Iraq was like for you. It's common to find yourself grappling with frustration. Don't act on it. Just keep plugging.

Things Ain't Normal

After my first trip to the Middle East, the most comforting thought on my return was my hope to resume normal routines with my spouse. This was not the case. In the months I was gone, she developed her own routines. I was not a part of them. It was frustrating, but again very normal, even healthy. She had to cope with her own day-to-day life and spouse-imposed fears.

You must be patient with your loved ones, your co-workers, and yourself. Do not bring a preconceived notion of normalcy home with you. Adapt to the "normal" you find when you return. That's harder than it sounds, and is actually more stressful than adapting to the danger of Iraq. After all, you *expected* to have to adjust to that; you thought going home was supposed to be easy.

What's Wrong with You

People in Iraq find themselves witnessing or participating in traumatic events. You may be nearby during horrific attacks, terrible accidents, and numerous situations where you find yourself and others under stressful and unpredictable conditions. The skills to deal with those situations do not come naturally.

You may find the friends you know best in Iraq suffer from acute stress, post-traumatic stress, or from being stressed out by all the stress around them. You yourself may be affected by one or all of these things.

You're Stressing, Dude

Acute stress is your body reacting up to a month later to life-threatening events—the gut-wrenchingly sudden, uncontrollable stuff that leaves you "scared @#$&-less" in the moment. Sexual assault can bring it on, or domestic violence, or natural disasters. An IED going off nearby is a lot like being in a sudden, terrible car wreck. Expect your body to respond the same way. It can leave you rattled for a couple of weeks.

Traumatic stress disorders come from the prolonged strain on the mind and body from repeated shocking or horrifying events. Any life-threatening incident experienced or witnessed will do. The effects can range from shock, to terror, to—and these are the big ones, kids—long-term irritability and dissociation from the "real" world.

You Don't Say

Final verse from The Eagles' 1976 hit "Hotel California":

*Last thing I remember, I was
Running for the door
I had to find the passage back
To the place I was before
'Relax,' said the night man,
We are programmed to receive.
You can check out any time you like,*

At the very least, you'll be burned out. We use the term *burnout* pretty liberally in the modern world. In Iraq, it is very real, the collective mental strain of working in a stressful environment. If you work a tough job in near isolation, if you are forced to be empathetic to everyone but yourself, if you put in long hours with few resources—in other words, if you work in Iraq—you can expect to get burned out.

A military study in 2004 looked at the mental health of troops who fought in Iraq and found that one in eight reported symptoms of post-traumatic stress disorder. Symptoms of major depression, anxiety, or PTSD were reported in *16 percent* of those in Iraq, compared to 11 percent of those who served in Afghanistan (where there was less combat), and 5 percent in the general U.S. population.

After being in Iraq, if you're like those soldiers, that means you can expect to *triple* the likelihood of becoming a basket case. I use this word respectfully. Your body is a remarkably adaptive machine. When you leave Iraq, you will notice how much it has adapted to living under stress.

Feeling spaced out, unable to concentrate, or exhausted—these are all lasting symptoms of traumatic stress. You may even wish you were going back, where at least you'll fit in with all these problems. This development will bother you most of all.

All of these feelings are normal.

Road to Wellsville

It may sound terrible, but psychologists tell us all of these things are survival mechanisms, and that they go away. The people who are best able to cope with returning to quieter life have a few traits in common:

- They focus on short time intervals while solving problems in their new (or old) lives.

- They place their traumatic experience into the context of full, meaningful lives.

- They appreciate their own competence and the support of others.

- They realize how traumatic events might continue to affect their life—long after the incident is over—and take steps to use the experience to their benefit.

Other psychologists have put their finger on how people convert traumas into valuable life lessons. ("Don't step on landmines," for instance. Just kidding.) They've discovered that people have to think through their own problems. Only the individual can do it, although research shows that intimates can help.

For the affected individual, the epiphany usually falls between two weeks and four months after the stressful event—and it is a sudden intuitive insight, rather than a drawn-out thinking process. Best of all, the realization helps the individual deal with later stressful situations.

So. Basket case? No way, my brothers and sisters. You're supermen. Still, you may need someone to point you away from the kryptonite. If you had nerve damage to your foot, you would see a specialist. Traumatic stress causes chemical injury in your brain. Get help. It's cool.

A good starting place is the National Center for Post-Traumatic Stress Disorder (www.ncptsd.va.gov). Your employer or health-care provider should have recommendations, too.

The Least You Need to Know

- Leaving Iraq is a bigger adjustment than arriving.
- You'll be amazed how clueless others are about Iraq.
- Your old pre-Iraq routine is gone; you'll have to adapt to a new one.
- If you are careful, physically and mentally, your Iraq experience will be fulfilling.

Networking and Getting Started

Don't just do something—sit there. Your designs of going to Iraq must fit into someone else's. But whose? And how do you connect with them? The resources to make those connections are in this appendix. Grab a sheet of paper and follow along.

1. What are your skills?

   ❏ Military   ❏ NGO
   ❏ Journalism   ❏ Engineer
   ❏ Public works   ❏ Electrical
   ❏ Plumber   ❏ Carpenter
   ❏ Other trade   ❏ Truck driver
   ❏ Food prep   ❏ Languages
   ❏ Medical   ❏ Communications
   ❏ Other

2. What projects/efforts would make the best use of your skills? Is your experience level sufficient to get these jobs in Iraq? How much personal risk are you willing to accept?

3. List companies operating in Iraq that are searching for your job skills, at your skill level.

4. Who in your business has been to Iraq, seen your work, and liked it? List their names and contact information.

Who else do you know that might refer you to someone else or be helpful otherwise? List friends, relatives, acquaintances, and business associates who have industry contacts.

5. List places you can go to network—job seminars, professional organizations, social gatherings, etc.

6. Prepare a resumé, and cover letter, contact the people identified in Steps 4 and 5, and send out feelers.

Good luck.

Job Websites

Jobs in Iraq can be found at the following places online, among other places. Their inclusion is not a recommendation:

General:

www.iraqijobcenter.com—Includes contracting jobs around the world

www.jobline.net/jobiraq1.htm—Offers paid job-hunting services

Some big contractors:

Kellogg, Brown & Root: www.halliburton.com/kbr

Parsons Corp.: www.parsons.com

Washington Group International:
www.wgint.com/opp_iraq.html

Bechtel: www.bechtel.com/iraq.htm

Current reconstruction contractors:

The U.S. Department of Commerce Iraq Investment
& Reconstruction Task Force website lists awarded
contracts and some subcontracts at www.export.gov/
iraq/market_ops/contracts03.html and www.export.
gov/iraq/market_ops/contracts04.html. Further
information on awarded contracts and grants may be
found at http://www.export.gov/Iraq/market_ops/
contracts.html.

Nongovernmental organization jobs:

United Nations Assistance Mission for Iraq:
www.uniraq.org/tools/vacancies.asp

Other NGO job postings: www.idealist.org.

Military recruiting:

www.military.com/Recruiting/Content/
0,13898,rec_splash,,00.html

www.defenselink.mil

Predeparture Checklist

You have a job in Iraq. All you need is a plan to get to it. If you haven't completed the following tasks already, you need to do so before leaving.

1. **Check the latest travel warnings for Iraq.**
    Most citizens of Western nations are permitted to travel to Iraq, though the U.S. State Department (and other governments) continues to warn against unnecessary travel.

    The State Dept.'s latest Travel Warning to Iraq can be found atwww.travel.state.gov/travel/iraq_warning.html.

    More information about security along *specific* routes or points of entry may be gleaned from private security firms working in Iraq. Ideally, you or your employer already has a contract with one. If so, you should be in frequent contact with them. If not, the U.S. State Department lists those working in Iraq online with their contact information at travel.state.gov/travel/iraq_securitycompanies.html. They are not in business to provide logistical services for free, but many will provide advice once or twice out of courtesy.

A final, inclusive resource for travelers to Iraq comes from the Iraq Investment and Reconstruction Task Force of the U.S. Department of Commerce, a must-check during planning: www.export.gov/iraq/bus_climate/travel_faq.html.

2. **Check the entry requirements that apply to you.** Requirements differ depending on whether you are a government employee, member of the military, contractor, or civilian traveling on business. (There are also tourist visas, but they may not be available at this time.) For U.S. citizens, check out the U.S. State Department's Consular Information Sheet for Iraq at www.travel.state.gov/travel/iraq.html. You can also look on the website of the U.S. Embassy in Baghdad at iraq.usembassy.gov. If you are not a citizen of the United States, similar information can be found by consulting with your own government and its consulate nearest to Iraq.

3. **Get a visa.** Rules for getting a visa are still evolving, and depend on whether you are working on a reconstruction contract. Contact the Iraqi embassy in Amman, Jordan, Washington, D.C., or nearest to your home before planning any trip to the region. The U.S. State Department's website (above) has information for U.S. citizens, and the website of the Iraqi embassy in Washington, D.C., also lists its requirements at consul. iraqiembassy.org.

Contacts for the nearest Iraqi embassy or consulate can be found at www.iraqmofa.net/index.aspx.

4. **Get immunized.** Some immunizations require multiple inoculations over a period of weeks. In addition to the measles and polio immunizations you probably received in childhood, you should consider getting immunized for Hepatitis A and B, tetanus, and diphtheria. A rabies inoculation is up to you, but feral dogs run wild all over Iraq.

   Full information is available at your local travel clinic, and at the U.S. Centers for Disease Control website (www.cdc.gov). Information on medical care in Iraq can be found online at the U.S. Embassy in Baghdad at iraq.usembassy.gov/iraq/citizen_services/medical_info.html. A list of public hospitals may be found at iraq.usembassy.gov/iraq/medical_facilities.html. Further and specific inquiries can be made through the following e-mail address: usconsulbaghdad@state.gov.

5. **Have the right equipment.** In addition to having clothing appropriate for the culture and climate, baggage for carrying it, and any indispensable personal items, you're going to need a helmet, bulletproof vest, and ballistic goggles capable of stopping flying debris.

   The Committee to Protect Journalists lists a number of protective gear companies at www.cpj.org/Briefings/2003/safety/contacts.html, as well as security companies that offer hostile environment training prior to leaving for Iraq.

Knowing how to handle yourself in a war zone should be considered a vital part of your mental equipment. Reading this book will not be enough. Here are profiles of some of the security companies listed by the CPJ:

- **AKE Ltd.** (www.akegroup.com). The name stands for "awareness, knowledge, and excellence." It's run by former British military people, including U.K. special forces. They provide security and training courses in the United States and United Kingdom that include situational awareness and combat first aid. Tel. (U.K.) +44 0 1432-267-111, (U.S.) +1 202 974-6556; E-mail: services@ake.co.uk.

- **Centurion Risk Assessment Services Ltd.** (www.centurion-riskservices.co.uk). Another firm run and taught by former British commandos. This firm offers a number of programs designed for getting by in war zones. Tel. +44 0 1264-355-255 or +44 0 7000-221-221; E-mail: main@centurion-riskservices.co.uk.

- **Objective Team Ltd.** (www.objectiveteam.com). A group run by former British intelligence officers that offers classes only in the United Kingdom. Tel. +44 0 1-788-899-029.

- **Pilgrims Group** (www.pilgrimsgroup.com). Run and taught by former British military types, Pilgrims is based in the United Kingdom, but also offers courses in the States. Pilgrims Group classes teach environmental awareness and emergency first aid. Tel. +44 0 1932-339-187; E-mail: training@pilgrimsgroup.com.

- **Travel Advisory Group Inc.** (www. traveladvisorygroup.com). A Virginia-based group run and taught by former members of the U.S. Navy Special Forces. E-mail: info@traveladvisorygroup.com.

6. **Arrange your trip to the region.** This should be done in coordination with your employer, and will probably involve a flight into Amman, Jordan, or Kuwait City, Kuwait. Again, with your employer's coordination, arrange for your hotel stay in a country neighboring Iraq. You may need a few days to a week to finish processing if your departure was hurried (as often happens with journalists).

7. **Check in on arrival.** U.S. citizens can find the nearest embassy or consulate through the U.S. State Department's travel registration website, travelregistration.state.gov. You can also register with the embassy by e-mailing usconsulbaghdad@state.gov, by telephone (+1 240 553-0584, ext. 5340 or 5635), or by calling their local cell phones at +964 7901 732 134, +964 7901 168 167, or +964 7901 168 383. The embassy is online at iraq. usembassy.gov and baghdad.usembassy.gov.

British citizens can reach their consulate by calling +964 7901 926 280 or +1 703 270 0254, by e-mail at britishconsulbaghdad@gtnet.gov.uk, or online at www.britishembassy.gov.uk/iraq.

Australians in Iraq should register with their embassy through the Department of Foreign Affairs and Trade at www.orao.dfat.gov.au. For urgent help, call the 24-hour Consular Emergency Centre in Canberra at +61 2 6261 3305. If you need to speak to a consular officer in Iraq, call mobile +1 914 360 3289 or fixed line +964 1 538 2100.

Good luck, and stay alert.

Planning Trips in Iraq

This appendix, along with Chapters 7 and 8, will help you plan the trips you must take while you are in the country.

The principles are to minimize your exposure to known risks, to get the job done quickly, and to get back safely.

The concepts you will apply spell APE: *awareness* of the dangers you must face, *probability* those risks will present themselves, and *evasion* of risks you can avoid.

The following tip sheet is adapted from those prepared for journalists. Courses in this material were taught by U.S. forces prior to the 2003 invasion of Iraq, and by private security firms at that time and since. Training through such a firm is essential; you should strongly consider contacting one of the ones mentioned in Appendix B, or one of the ones currently working in Iraq listed by the U.S. State Department at travel. state.gov/travel/iraq_securitycompanies.html.

Why are you undertaking this trip? What risks might you face along the way? Can you overcome those risks?

Begin by updating your knowledge of the area's recent background:

- Who is fighting in the area, and what is their current *modus operandi?*

- Who lives in the area where you are going, and will any ethnic, religious, language, or cultural differences complicate your job?

- Are there any easily identifiable dangers specific to this area, including disease?

- How long will you need to be there—and to reduce exposure, what's the shortest amount of time that you need to accomplish your job?

Next consider the equipment you'll need:

- Is there anything special you'll need to accomplish the task?

- Is there anything special you'll need for your own safety?

- Do you have the first-aid kit, the car-repair equipment, the maps, and the communications gear you'll need?

- Are you dressed appropriately for climate and local culture?

- Will you or someone with you be armed? Is this a good idea or a bad idea?

Finally, think about your "what-ifs." Everyone traveling with you will need to be on the same page in the event of common snafus.

The most typical include the mundane—a traffic accident or breakdown, a communications foul-up, or traffic delays—but may also include a medical emergency or attack typical for the current threats in the area where you'll be traveling.

Agree ahead of time when you'll give up on the day's plan and head for home.

And update your plans throughout your trip. Good communication is essential.

Appendix D

Important Iraqi Phrases

The Arabic dialect spoken in Iraq is distinctive from those spoken in Egypt, Palestine, and the Persian Gulf region. Just like anyone, Iraqis appreciate the efforts of foreigners to learn the native tongue. Here are the basics.

Basics and Being Polite

English	Iraqi Arabic
Yes	naam/ay (pronounced like the letter A)
No	la
Maybe	inshallah (if God wills)
Not	muu
Please	tfaddil (m)/tfaddlich (f) /tfaddlkum (p)
	min fadlak (m)/-ich (f)/-kum (p)
Please (to request)	allay-khall-ak (m)/-ich (f)/-kum (p) *The "kh" sound is pronounced like the scratchy "ch" in the Scottish "loch."*
Help me	sah-id-nee
Please, help me.	allay-khallak, sah-id-nee.
Thank you	shukran

English	Iraqi Arabic
With pleasure	bikull suruur
I	anee
You	inta (m)/ inti (f)
You (pl)	intu
We	iHna
They	humma
I'm well.	anee nzein
I'm a Canadian.	anee canadee.
Excuse me	(to m) ahn idhnak
	The "dh" sound is pronounced like the hard "th" in the English "that."
	(to f) ahn idhnich
	(to p) ahn idhkum
Hello	marhaba
Peace be with you.	salaam alay-kum
	(reply) alay-kum ah-salaam
Good morning	sabaa al-khair
	(reply) Sabba hih-nuur
English	**Iraqi Arabic**
Good afternoon	masah ala-khair
	(reply) masa al-nuur
Good night	(to m) tisbah ala-khair
	(to f) tisbaheen ala-khair
	(to p) tisbahuun ala-khair
How are you?	(to m) shlawnak?
	(to f) shlawnich?
	(to p) shlawnkum?
Good	n-zein
	bikheer

Bad   muu-n-zein
Praise be to God   al-ham-doo-lillah
Thank God   nushkur allah
What's up?   shaku maku?
Not much.   maku shii.
Goodbye   ma-ah-salaama
                            fii amman-oo-lah
See you   ashufak (m)/-ich (f)/-kum (p)

Questions and Conjunctions

Who?   minu?
What?   shnu?
When?   shwakit?
Where?   wain?
Why?   lesh?
How?   shlawn?
How do you know?   shmadriik? (m) /-ich (f)/ -kum (p)
How many?   kam?
How much? (buying)   beesh? ibbeesh?
How long?   shgadd?
Whose?   maalman?
Where from?   imeen?, mneen?
Truly?   ballah?
Isn't it?   muu ballah?
What'd you think?   sh 'aball-ak (m)/-ich (f)/ -kum (p)
Where've you been?   haay wain?
And   w (wuh)
But   bass
Or   wallah

Airport Words

Airport	mah-tar
Luggage	junta
Here	henna
There	hin-nock
There is/are	aku
There isn't/aren't	maku
Passport	bassbort
My passport	bassbort-ee
Here's (my passport)	tfaddal haadha (bassbortee)
Your passport	bassbort-ak (m)/ -ich (f)
American	amriiki (m)/ -iyyah (f)
British	inglizi (m)/ -iyyah (f)
With you? (Do you have?)	mah-ak(m)/ -ich (f)
I have	ahndee
I don't have	maa ahndee
With me (I have)	mah-ee
This	hadha
These	hadhoola
Customs inspector	mufattish
Clothes	malabbis
Everything	kullha
Camera	gahmira
Cigarettes	jigahyeer
Taxi	tahksi
Car	siyyarrah

Hotel Words

Hotel	findig
House	bait
Receptionist	mudayyif
Hotel reservation	hajiz bil-findig
How long will you be staying?	kam yoom bahk-yah?
I'm staying	anee bahk-yah
A week	usboo
Two weeks	usbain
A day	al-yoom
Welcome	ahlan w-sahlan
	(reply) ahlan beek
Sir	hadirtak
Ma'am	hadirtich
Room/s	goorfah/goo-raaf
Ready	hadra
Key	al-miftaah
Bathroom	hammaam
Hot	hahr
Cold	baareed
Window	shoo-BOTCH

Numbers

Number/s	ragam/argaam
0	sifir
1	wahid
2	thneen

3	thalaatha
4	arbah
5	khamsa
6	sittah
7	sabah
8	thamaaniyah
9	tis-ah
10	ash-rah
11	ih-dashar
12	thnash
13	thalaath-ashar
14	arbaat-ashar
15	khamst-ashar
16	sitt-ashar
17	sabaht-ashar
18	thamant-ashar
19	tis-ah-ashar
20	ish-reen
21	wahid w-ishreen
30	tlaatheen
40	arabah-een
50	khamseen
60	sitteen
70	sab-een
80	thmaaneen
90	tis-een
100	miyyah
101	miyyah w-wahid
200	mittain
300	thalaath miyyah
1,000	alif
2,000	alfain
One million	milyoon

Telling Time

What time is it?	beesh is-sah-uh?
It's (telling time)...	As-sah-uh
1 o'clock.	...wahid.
It's 9 o'clock.	As-sah-uh tis-ah.
...1:15	...wahid w roo-buh
	(one and a quarter)
...1:20	...wahid w thilith
...1:30	...wahid w nuss
...1:35	...wahid w nuss w khamsa
	(one, and a half, and five)
...1:25	...wahid w nuss illa khamsa
	(one, and a half, less five)
...quarter to two	...ithnain illa rubuh
...twenty to two	...ithnain illa thilith
What day is it?	shnu al-yoom?
Today is...	al-yoom ...
Sunday	yoom al-wahid
Monday	yoom li-thnain
Tuesday	yoom ith-thalaathah
Wednesday	yoom al-arbah
Thursday	yoom al-khamec
Friday	yoom al-joom-ah
Saturday	yoom as-sabbit
Month	shahar

Calendar

English	Arabic	Eastern Calendar
January	yanayeer	kaanuun ith-thanee
February	fabraayeer	shbaat
March	maaris	adhaar
April	abreel	nees-ahn
May	may-oo	ayyar
June	yoonyoo	huzayrahn
July	yoolyoo	tammooz
August	ughustus	ahb
September	sibtambar	aylool
October	uktoobar	tishreen il-awwal
November	noovambar	tishreen il-thaanee
December	deesambar	kaanoon il-awwal

Food

Hungry	ju-ahn
I'm hungry	anee ju-ahn
Are you hungry?	inta ju-ahn?
Are they hungry?	humma ju-ah-neen?
Food	akul
Eastern food	akul sharqi
Western food	akul gharbi

Family

Family	ahal
How's the family?	shloon lahal?
They're fine.	humma bkheer, al-ham-doo-lillah.
Husband	zawj
Wife	zawja
Mother	umm
Father	ab
Father of (in a name)	Abu ...
Mother of (in a name)	Umm ...
Uncle	khaal (maternal)
	'ahmm (paternal)
Aunt	khaala (maternal)
	'ahmma (paternal)
Child, son	weled (boy)
Children	awled (boys and girls)
Girl, daughter	bint
Girls	binaat
Grandmother	jidda
Grandfather	jidd
Grandchild	hafiid

Suggested Reading

Modern Iraq

The Iraq War Reader; History, Documents, Opinions ed. Michah L. Sifry and Christopher Cerf (Simon & Schuster, 2003)

The Old Social Classes and the Revolutionary Movements of Iraq: Third Edition, by Hanna Batatu (Saqi Books, 2004)

A History of Iraq, by Charles Tripp (Cambridge University Press, 2002)

Republic of Fear: The Politics of Modern Iraq, Updated Edition, by Kanan Makiya (University of California Press, 1998)

The Making of Iraq, 1900–1963: Capital, Power, and Ideology, by Samira Haj (State University of New York Press, 1997)

Iraq: A Country Study, 4th Edition, ed. Helen Chapin Metz (U.S. Department of the Army, 1990)

Future Iraq: US Policy in Reshaping the Middle East, by Geoff Simons (Saqi Books, 2004)

Middle East

The Essential Middle East: A Comprehensive Guide, by Dilip Hiro (Carroll & Graf Publishers, 2003)

A History of the Arab Peoples, by Albert Hourani (Warner Books, 1992)

Bedouin Tribes of the Euphrates, by Anne Blunt (Cass, 1968)

Ancient Mesopotamia

The Legacy of Mesopotamia, ed. Stephanie Dalley (Oxford University Press, 1998)

Ancient Iraq, 3rd Edition, by Georges Roux (Penguin Books, 1993)

Twin Rivers: A Brief History of Iraq from the Earliest Times to the Present Day, by Seton Lloyd (H. Milford, Oxford University Press, 1943)

Iraqi Arabic

Modern Iraqi Arabic, A Textbook, by Yasin M. Alkalesi (Georgetown University Press, 2001)

A Dictionary of Iraqi Arabic, ed. Beverly Clarity, Karl Stowasser, Ronald G. Wolfe, D. R. Woodhead, and Wayne Beene (Georgetown University Press, 2003)

Gulf Arabic, by Jack Smart and Frances Altorfer, (Teach Yourself Books, 1999)

Index

W-X-Y-Z